THE
STORY ⚙ WORKS
Guide to Writing
POINT OF VIEW

Alida Winternheimer

for my students
past, present, and future

Get Your Bonus

Thank you for picking up *The Story Works Guide to Writing Point of View*.

Please visit www.WordEssential.com/JoinStoryWorksPOV.

You'll receive a downloadable Choose the Right Point of View Character worksheet to help you keep your characters in the game. To learn more about when to use which point of view character see chapter nine.

You'll also:

- receive Alida's writing tips newsletter and the Story Works Round Table podcast,
- be notified when future books in The Story Works Guide to Writing Fiction Series come out,
- be the first to hear about writing courses, and
- get special offers.

Don't forget the cool factor!

The question is not what you
look at, but what you see.

~ Henry David Thoreau

Contents

Foreword

How do you make a story come alive? How do you generate emotion using description? How do you create a sweeping epic that spans decades and nations, or a claustrophobic tale of horror that is restricted to a single room and a single hour? How do you render a character who can never be forgotten? The answer, to all of these questions, is point of view. It is the heart and soul of storytelling.

Most new writers write in whatever style feels comfortable and familiar to them. They use the point of view that they read or enjoy the most. But it is vital to tailor your point of view to the type of story you want to write. You wouldn't wear a wedding dress to play rugby, and you shouldn't try to write an intimate character sketch in omniscient or an epic fantasy in first person. Alida Winternheimer's *The Story Works Guide to Writing Point of View* will show you how to create the *best* point of view to tell the story you need to tell.

I met Alida in early 2010. I sat next to her during our first class for our Master of Fine Arts in Creative Writing at Hamline University. I was lucky to have met her. She was and is a fierce friend and a brilliant colleague. Her editorial insight is flawless. Her writing draws me in, keeps me glued to the page, and, occasionally, gives me nightmares! If I am ever stuck with a particularly thorny issue of craft, I turn immediately to Alida. When I have a new manuscript, she is the first to get a glimpse. She is one of the few people in the world that I trust with my writing.

Since graduating with my MFA, I have gone on to teach point of view multiple times, so I feel qualified to give you a few pointers as you work through this book. First, I recommend paying close attention to the definitions in chapter two. Alida takes confusing terminology and makes it clear and easy to follow. Return to chapter two as often as needed! Second, do the exercises in each chapter. This may seem obvious, but too often writers skip the exercises in craft books. Make an exception for *The Story Works Guide to Writing Point of View*. The exercises are well thought out, straightforward, and easy to follow. More importantly, they brilliantly reinforce the lessons learned in each chapter. Trust me, you'll be better off for it. And trust Alida. I know I have, and I've never regretted it.

Nicodemus Wolfgang Taranovsky
St. Paul, Minnesota
April 19, 2017

Introduction

When it comes to using point of view in fiction, I've come across two types of writers: those that agonize over the correct point of view for their story, weighing the pros and cons of first person, of omniscient versus close third, with careful scrutiny before they begin putting words on the page...and those that choose a point of view instinctively, without thinking, relying on their guts to guide them.

The first type of writer is almost too aware of point of view as the subtle element of craft that it is. They consider every option. They agonize over the implications of a certain choice, scout out the hazards and label potential pitfalls with regards to plot, backstory, and emotional connectivity. Will first person point of view be easier to relate to? Will the omniscient be hard to connect with?

The second type of writer is blissfully unaware, like a bull in a china shop, charging into the story without stopping to question what they are doing. Choosing a point of view, for them, might be as simple as going with what they are used to reading.

Being one type is as good as the other. In fact, no two writers are ever the same. We all have to start from where we are and improve from there.

Still, as writers advance in their genres, it's only natural to become more aware of point of view as an element of choice in their craft, and therefore more considered in their choice when it comes to how they use point of view in their stories.

Fortunately for beginning and advanced writers everywhere, no matter where you are in your mastery of the craft (or what you *think* you've mastered—there's always something new to learn, isn't there?), this thorough and deeply nuanced guide to point of view, written by seasoned writer and editor Alida Winternheimer, is bound to help you take your craft to new levels.

Those of you that already agonize over point of view decisions have in front of you the definitive guide to point of view you've always wanted. Not only will Alida be able to teach you how to improve your handle on first and third person and every variation between, but you will also find that her lessons help take some of the fear and pain out of this part of the writing process by helping you understand why to make certain choices, how to avoid common pitfalls in the many varieties of point of view, and how to use your own strengths to your advantage.

For the other type of writer, the bulls out there, Alida will educate and inform you. You don't know what you don't know, after all. Here's your master class. A great freedom comes from knowing your options. Even if you want to continue charging around at the whim of your instincts (and why not, if it's brought you this far?) you'll now do so with a well of wisdom to return to if trashing the china shop ever comes back to bite you in the butt.

I, myself, fell into the second camp, the bull's camp. But with guidance and gentle eye opening from Alida, I've slowly begun to expand my point of view choices. With every book I write, I consider point of view more deeply, and it has helped me connect with readers in ways that bring me joy every day.

No matter where you start, one thing I hope you take away from *The Story Works Guide to Writing Point of View* is that this aspect of craft will allow you to connect with readers in a deep and fundamental way. Point of view is the vehicle through which that connection is made possible in fiction.

Now come along and learn more about point of view. No matter where you are in your journey, improve your mastery of point of view and your readers will thank you for it.

Matt Herron
Austin, Texas
April 30, 2017

Chapter 1

How to Use This Book

A NOTE FROM ALIDA

Thank you for picking up *The Story Works Guide to Writing Point of View*.

Writing is an infamously solitary pursuit. We need to concentrate on our words and slip away from reality into an imagined world where our creations work, fight, and play. Writing that world is a journey. Like most journeys, a good friend makes the effort more enjoyable. I designed this book to be a resource to come back to whenever you have a question about point of view and narrative voice. I hope it will feel like a reliable friend.

This book is a companion and sequel to *The Story Works Guide to Writing Character*. You do not need to have read that book first, but you may find it beneficial, because character, point of view, and narrative voice are intrinsically bound together. Perhaps that essential nature is what makes point of view so full of intricacies.

By the time you've gone through this book and its exercises, you'll have a solid grasp of those inevitable and imperative aspects of story. And with that, you'll be ready to play with those voices, opening up new avenues of invention in your creative writing.

Though we may never meet, every text is a conversation between the author, the text, and all of its readers. Here begins our conversation about point of view and narrative voice. I'm excited to get started. You may not be excited. You may be anxious, like on the first day of a new class. However you feel, it's all right. Grab your tea or coffee. Your notebook and pencil. And get comfortable. We're going to talk craft. I'm sure it'll be fun, but if there is one thing I can geek out about, it's story craft. You can find me online easily enough, and, if you like, we can continue this conversation long after you finish the book. Maybe you'll even geek out with me.

WHAT YOU'LL GET FROM THIS BOOK

Story is obviously composed of character, plot, and setting. Point of view is a less obvious but equally essential aspect of story—without it no story would exist. Point of view is profound, yet we are so used to encountering it as readers that we are hardly aware of it, let alone able to define it. That would be like asking the proverbial fish to define water. In these pages, I will show you how to create a well-crafted point of view that is both powerful and subtle. You'll learn how to select the *best* point of view for your story, discover the vital connection between your narrator and point of view character, understand the role of narrative in any story, learn how to determine if your point of view character is qualified to also be a first person narrator, and more.

I have organized the chapters so that there is a logical flow to the material and each chapter builds on those before it.

- Chapters one through three provide your introduction to the large and sometimes overwhelming topic of point of view.
- Chapters four and five introduce you to your new best friend, the narrator, and help you understand his role and how distance functions in your story.
- Chapters six and seven should convince you of the importance and primacy of narrative point of view in any story.
- Chapters eight through eleven deal with the specifics of person, with a chapter dedicated to each: third, multiple, omniscient, and first person.
- Chapters twelve through fifteen go deep into special topics, like the unreliable narrator and info dumps.

In each chapter, you will find plenty of excerpts that provide practical examples to study and compare. There are nineteen exercises that will change how you approach point of view. These exercises work for whatever story you're developing right now, and you can repeat these exercises every time you create a new story.

Chapter two is a primer on point of view to introduce you to the terminology I'll be using throughout the book. The terms are those we've inherited from the literary canon. As such, they are long established and (mostly) well defined. If some of them seem like stuffed shirts, give them a chance. They might be old fashioned, but they will play an important role in our conversation about point of view.

At the end of each chapter is a Recap section you can use as reference material. The final chapter is titled "Problems with Point of View (And How to Fix Them)" and is another reference tool for when you need that one specific solution to your point of view problem. At the back of the book, there is a glossary of key terms and where to find them in the text. Each glossary term is italicized when it appears with its definition. There is also a list of the exercises in this book and their locations.

Deciding your story's point of view needs to be done in the prewriting stage of development. This is because changing the point of view of a story after you've got a draft well under way is a total *pain in the butt.*

I recommend you approach the exercises in this book as prewriting development. If you ever decide you need to change a story's point of view, take heart. You are not the first writer to do so, and your story will surely benefit from the shift.

THE CREATIVE POWER OF PREWRITING BY HAND

If you search "handwriting and creativity" online, you'll find plenty of articles about the benefits of handwriting and concern over its disappearance from our culture and elementary curriculums. One study by Virginia Berninger, a psychologist at the University of Washington, demonstrated that printing, cursive writing, and typing on a keyboard are all associated with distinct and separate brain patterns. When subjects composed text by hand, they consistently produced more words and expressed more ideas. Brain imaging suggested that the connection between writing and idea generation went even further. The subjects with better handwriting exhibited greater neural activation in areas associated with working memory and increased overall activation in the reading and writing networks (Konnikova, Maria. "What's Lost as Handwriting Fades." *New York Times*, June 2, 2014). There is also plenty of anecdotal evidence from writers to be found in conversations, interviews, blogs, etc., professing that grabbing a pen is often critical to the creative process, whether that's generating a first draft or stepping away from the keyboard to get unstuck.

You don't have to believe me. Get a journal for the exercises in this book. As you do them, exercise your fine motor control by putting pen to paper—and watch your creativity get a boost!

RULES

The rules of point of view are more rigid than in other areas of craft. That is because they shape the foundation of any story. Once they are established—and establishing them is up to *you*—they should never be violated. They are the frame of your house. And with the house framed, you can build anything you want using your characters, plot, and setting to make your home unique. Gambrel roof? Spanish tile? Greek columns? Build away!

I gladly acknowledge that there are exceptions to every rule and circumstances where bending the rule is the best thing you could do.

Exceptions and rule bending must be examined on a case-by-case basis, which is beyond the scope of this book.

THE EXAMPLES IN THIS BOOK

I use examples from my own work. That's because I can both analyze them and explain my choices as the writer. Also, I own the material, so there's no concern with copyright.

A good number of my editing and coaching clients have given me permission to use their work as examples in this series of books. When you see an excerpt that is not from my work, it's from one of these brave writers. I am finding it easy to use positive examples, but these writers gave their permission with the understanding that I might excerpt a work in progress to point out what not to do, and I am indebted to them for their trust. There are links at the back of the book so you can find their work. Please do.

SKILLS AND CONFIDENCE

You will come away from reading this book with an understanding of point of view and how it functions in any story. You will have the skills to craft your story's point of view with control and confidence.

The Story Works Guide to Writing Fiction Series exists to help you write better stories, for yourself, for your stories, for your readers.

May you grow as a storyteller, and may your every point of view be earned.

Chapter 2

Point of View Primer

THE ESTABLISHED TERMINOLOGY

To get a handle on point of view, you need to know what to call its various moving parts. And I do mean moving, because you can combine them in any way you can imagine—so long as you do it well.

Please don't feel like you need to memorize the terminology. You won't be quizzed. Read through this chapter so you can familiarize yourself with the terms I'll be using throughout the book. The more comfortable you are with the words, the better. If you retain things by taking notes—like me—go ahead and start a new entry in your craft journal. These terms will be reintroduced and used in the chapters ahead with lots of discussion and examples; however, if you need a refresher on the terminology later, return to this chapter.

Welcome to the canon.

The terminology used in describing point of view combine to define how the narrator relates to the point of view character and the reader. This in turn will define how the author expects the reader to relate to the story.

Point of View: When we discuss point of view, we mean the narrative constructs, or conceptual elements, through which a story is told to a reader. We refer to the narrative as a whole, which include the roles of the author, the narrator, and the point of view character, as well as abstract concepts like omniscience and distance.

Point of view (and this book) is about far more than your point of view character. It is about the very warp and weft of the fabric of your story. Throughout this book, "point of view" will refer to the totality of point of view. When I refer to a character, I will specify "the point of view character."

Narrator/Narrative Voice/Authorial Voice: This is the teller of the story. *Every* story has a narrator.

Sometimes the narrator is a character in the story, but more often the narrator is the voice of the author as God or the author's persona speaking to the reader from behind the covers of the book, invisible but always present.

Types of Narrator
1. Omniscient: This means the author plays God. The narrator is all-knowing, all-seeing, and all-reporting. The narrator can be anywhere

and shows the reader anything useful to advancing the story at any point in the story's chronology. The narrator can also report details from outside the time and space of the story. For example, the narrator could tell us something about a character's great-grandchild, who won't be born for decades after the close of the story. The omniscient narrator can also enter nonhuman perspectives, like the land or a table.

1A. Authorial-Omniscient: This is an unnamed, formal, invisible narrator found in the classic form of narrative. The storyteller is all-knowing, all-seeing, and can enter any head she wants to. This narrator has the weighty presence of God and always speaks the truth. The authorial-omniscient narrative voice may be applied to any number of heads in a story, including a single point of view. She *can* enter any head, but she does not exercise this power unless it is the best choice for the story.

If your narrator is godlike, she is a benevolent, impartial, all-knowing, all-seeing witness to and reporter of the story. She tells the good and bad for the benefit of the reader without passing judgment. Judgment is for the reader, not the narrator.

1B. Essayist-Omniscient: This narrator is the author's persona, or ethos. The author invents a persona to insert between himself and the reader as the teller of the story. The narrator may be a character with a relationship, however distant, to the characters and events of the story, or an unnamed, invisible storyteller who has a personality that comes through in the voice of the piece. An author who uses the essayist-omniscient narrator may invent a distinct voice for each story he writes.

If your narrator is an essayist, he is allowed to express his opinion on the matters he reports (as in op-ed pieces), unlike a journalist ("Just the facts, ma'am"). He is also allowed to have a personality and express it, unlike God. The essayist-omniscient narrator is the author's persona—his agent—not the author himself.

2. Third Person Narrator: In a third person narrative, the narrator refers to the point of view character in the third person, as he, Bill, or she, Nancy.

2A. Limited Third Person: The limited narrator is *limited* to the information available to the point of view character. The limited third person narrative is far more common than the omniscient.

2B. Close/Subjective Third Person: In a limited, close point of view, the focus and emphasis is on that character's experiences, knowledge, and thoughts—a subjective point of view—hence the similarity between close third and first person narratives. This has been the predominant point of view in modern literature for decades.

"Close third" or "close third person" is a common designation for this point of view. "Subjective third" is seldom encountered.

2C. Objective Third Person: The objective narrator is limited to external, observable facts and dialogue, like a camera. The narrator never enters a character's head nor reports anything beyond what is observed and observable.

The objective narrator is seldom used. Ernest Hemingway's short story, "Hills Like White Elephants," is an example of an objective point of view.

3. First Person Narrator: The main character tells his own story, functioning both as actor and narrator.

> **3A. Central First Person:** The first person narrator is at the center of the action.

> **3B. Peripheral First Person:** The first person narrator is not the central figure of the story, but a witness and reporter.

Point of View Character: This refers to the character who is ascribed the point of view of the story. It is this character's perspective through which we experience the events of the story. The reader will be expected to identify with this character over all others as she reads the story. The point of view character must be forever changed by the events of the story.

Distance: The term distance has a twofold meaning, referring to both the narrator's and the reader's relationship to the characters and events of the story. The narrator controls distance by manipulating what is shown and how it is presented to the reader. There are several shades of distance we'll be discussing in this book.

1. Physical Distance: The narrative lens functions like the lens on a camera, framing the scene presented to the reader, increasing or decreasing the sense of spatial distance between the reader and the action. Think of a camera zooming out when the distance is great and zooming in when the distance is small.

2. Emotional Distance: This refers to the degree to which the narrator engages with the point of view character's perspective. When the distance is close, the narrator maintains close alignment with the point of view character's perspective, essentially showing the reader the story through the point of view character's eyes. When the distance is middle or distant, the narrator has more freedom to present aspects of the story that do not align with the point of view character's perspective on the story's events.

3. Psychic Distance: This refers to the degree to which the reader engages emotionally with the point of view character's perspective. When the distance is close, there is typically more evocative content that encourages the reader to identify with or feel opposition to the character.

Note: Not all scholars will distinguish between emotional and psychic distance. You may find the terms used interchangeably by one writer, while another uses only one term or the other. For our purposes, it will be useful to make a distinction between them. Emotional distance refers to the sense of distance between the *narrator* and the point of view character. Psychic distance refers to the sense of distance between the *reader* and the point of view character. Keep in mind that emotional distance causes psychic distance, because the narrator presents the story to the reader with the effects of distance in mind.

4. Chronological Distance: This phrase refers to the amount of time that has passed between the events of the story and its telling. It places the character as narrator on a timeline after the events of the story have passed.

Identification and Opposition: How you shape distance in your story will affect the reader's engagement with your point of view character. This can be placed on a spectrum between identification and opposition, or acceptance and rejection of the character as a (pretend) human being.

If your head is spinning a little, don't worry. These terms will be defined again and explored in depth in the chapters ahead. You can turn back here at any time to refresh your grasp of the vocabulary.

The great thing is that if you've ever written a story, you've already put some or all of these elements of point of view to use. With each page you read, these concepts will become less abstract and more practical. And *that* is why this is a guide and not a discussion of theory.

Chapter 3

What Is Point of View?

IT'S MORE THAN A CHARACTER THINKING OUT LOUD

Point of view (commonly referred to as POV) is possibly the most important element of story craft for any writer to understand. Your story is defined by your point of view.

I do not mean your point of view *character* defines your story. The point of view character is one element of the point of view of a literary work. When writers have conversations about a story and reference its point of view, they typically discuss the character, but it is a mistake to think the character carries the entire story. He does not and cannot.

Likewise, your narrator (or narrative voice or authorial voice) is part of point of view. Your narrator and point of view character are separate entities the same way your left hand and right hand are separate entities. You could function with only one, but you are meant to have both, and life is better when they work together.

The narrator is your necessary middleman. It is the narrator who tells the story to the reader. It is the narrator who enters a character's point of view for the sake of the reader's experience. Narrator and point of view character are BFFs. They need each other. And your reader needs them both.

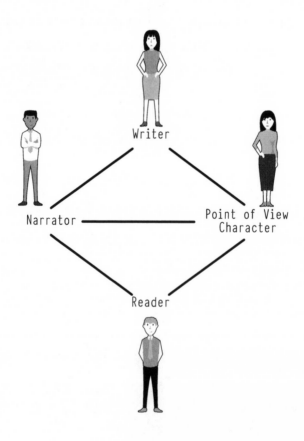

WORD ONE: POINT OF VIEW

Your story's point of view is the first thing a reader encounters, whether aware of it or not, and it defines the shape of your story. Point of view is something you had better decide on early in the writing process and stick with your decision. If you have to change the point of view of your book—and plenty of writers have—you're looking at rewriting *everything*. Point of view is more than pronoun choice and number agreement. You cannot simply use a "find and replace" command to switch all occurrences of "I" to "she." Everything in every scene must align with your point of view, from the sentence structure to the perspective of the point of view character. By doing a little work now, you'll avoid a painful rewrite later.

> That old saying, an ounce of prevention is worth a pound of cure, is worth remembering as you work through the exercises ahead. And when you finish them all, congratulate yourself on a job well done!

Point of view is, simply put, the narrative constructs, or conceptual elements, through which a reader experiences the story. The *point of view character* provides the perspective through which a reader has a specific, personal experience of the story's events. Now let's talk about the elements of point of view that shape any and every story.

BASIC ELEMENTS OF POINT OF VIEW

Point of view consists of four basic elements:

- Person: first, second, third;
- Tense: past, present;
- Number: single, multiple, omniscient; and
- Distance: close, middle, distant.

The point of view of a story is identified by terminology such as close first, multiple third, distant third, and omniscient. When describing a point of view, I will use commas between the various terms to serve as a visual reminder of the different elements. For example, a "third person, past tense, multiple, close point of view." Because stories are more often in the past tense, writers might leave past tense to be inferred and only mention if a story is present tense. Conversationally, we might describe the same story as a "multiple close third."

> These terms identify how the author has handled the combination of the story's narrative elements and the main character's perspective.

Person is identified by the pronoun used in the story's narrative. "I stepped outside," is a first person singular narrative. "We stepped outside," is a first person plural narrative; the point of view is a collective character. Plural person narratives are rare. "You stepped outside," is second person, and could refer to a single or plural point of view. "He stepped outside," is third person singular. "They stepped outside," is third person plural, referring to a collective character. Again, plural person narratives are rare.

Jeffrey Eugenides's *The Virgin Suicides* is an example of a first person plural point of view. While the characters making up the point of view are distinct individuals—a group of neighborhood boys infatuated with a group of sisters—the narrative refers to them as a collective consciousness, a "we."

Tense simply identifies whether a story is told in the past or present tense. "I went" versus "I go." Past tense is the standard, so much so that writers who work in the present tense will find themselves slipping into the past without realizing it.

Number refers to how many perspectives the narrator can enter over the course of the story. A single point of view means we only experience one character's perspective. A multiple point of view means we experience two or more characters' perspectives. An omniscient point of view means the narrator can enter *all* the characters' perspectives. Omniscient narrators refer to characters in the third person.

Omniscient also means the narrator is, just like God, not bound by the laws of space or time. He can flash forward and backwards beyond the lifetime of characters, can relate one character's experience to another's in ways the characters themselves cannot, and can even enter the perspective of the setting, the props, and the universe at large. An excellent example of an omniscient novel is Edward P. Jones's *The Known World.*

Distance generally refers to the emotional and psychic distance. When we talk about emotional distance, we mean the sense of distance between the narrator and the point of view character. When we talk about the psychic distance, we mean the sense of distance between the reader and the point of view character.

Conversationally, writers seldom distinguish between emotional and psychic distance, because they are *nearly* the same thing. If the emotional distance is distant, the psychic distance is most likely distant as well. I am making the distinction here for our purpose of studying narrative craft.

In a first person narrative, chronological distance affects emotional distance—time heals all wounds—so the chronological and emotional distances are typically inseparable. A narrator can tell the story as it occurs and still establish emotional distance—just as you can know a person who is dispassionate, stoic, and barely emotive.

These and other aspects of distance will be covered in detail in the chapter five, "Don't Stand So Close to Me."

WHAT ABOUT LIMITED?

Limited is a term I seldom use to describe a point of view. The reason is it's superfluous. If you are writing in a close third, the term limited is implied. If you are writing in first person, limited is implied. As far as your narrator is concerned, it is an either-or situation. If she is not omniscient, she is limited. In a *limited point of view*, the narrator's knowledge, and therefore her capacity to report information to the reader, is limited to what the point of view character can know.

Regardless of number, of how many characters' heads your narrator enters, said narrator will either be omniscient or limited. If your narrator is limited, she can only know what her point of view character(s) can know.

Can is the operative word here. Your narrator must show the reader far more than the point of view character is aware of at any given moment. Think of the story's narrative like the camera on a movie set. The camera can show the audience more than the character sees, but not more than is *available* to see in that moment. The face at the window? The character *could* notice the face, but is oblivious to it, so the narrator describes it for the reader.

If you are being true to your story's point of view, then your narrator will be appropriately knowledgeable and, conversely, appropriately limited. The key is consistency. Establish your rules and abide by them.

HELLO, WORLD

You enter a world that is different from your own each time you read a story, much like traveling somewhere new. But even in an unfamiliar place, the people and surroundings can feel familiar and comfortable—or not. In a story, whether something is familiar or comfortable will depend on how your point of view character sees the world around her, how she interacts with it, and how she judges it. A reader will experience the world on the page through and along with that character. As the writer, be aware that how your point of view character experiences a scenario will shape how your reader experiences it.

Here's an example to illustrate.

Anne was exhausted from two full days of travel—Minneapolis, Chicago, London, and finally Harare, Zimbabwe—but she was also excited. The sleep-deprived, adrenaline-fueled, wired kind of excited. Six months of study abroad in sub-Saharan Africa was the sort of experience people described as life changing. Of course it would be life changing; how could it not be? But *how* would it change her life? That remained to be seen, and she couldn't wait to find out.

Anne's host mother, whom she called Amai, Shona for mother, stood at the electric range in the kitchen, stirring a large pot with a big wooden spoon. A short woman with a close-cut afro, Amai was quiet but warm. She favored long skirts and short-sleeved blouses. When she moved through the house, the *slap slap* of her rubber flip-flops over tile flooring made her whereabouts known. "Here, Annie, you stir the *sadza.*"

Anne took the spoon from Amai and began to stir the pot, but the spoon stuck. "Oh my gosh." She gripped the long handle with both hands and pushed the spoon through the pot of thickened corn meal. "It's so hard," she said, surprised that she, hardly a weakling, could barely move the spoon around the pot.

Amai chuckled. "No. It is not hard. You need to get strong. Stay and cook with me every night, then we'll get you strong."

Amai and her family lived in a rambler in a nice neighborhood. All of the houses on the street were similar in size and shape with cream or beige walls and red tile roofs. Nice yards landscaped with palm trees were enclosed by five-foot cinderblock walls with broken bottle glass cemented to the top. Green shards glowed brightly in the hot sun, like a deadly confection topping the dull gray walls. Every window and door had bars on it. Anne assumed that the security measures were left over from Zimbabwe's recent colonial history. She never felt unsafe at Amai's, except for the brief occasions when she allowed herself to imagine a house fire she would never be able to escape. In fact, other than the bars and broken glass, Amai's neighborhood reminded her of her grandmother's in Las Vegas, Nevada.

Anne is clearly a stranger in a strange land, but how does she feel about this place? Is it familiar? Is it comfortable? How familiar and comfortable does it feel to you, the reader? How much of that has to do with your own experience and how much Anne's perspective?

Let's look at another example.

Anne's Chiweshe host father, Baba Kapeta, was the only person in his family who spoke more than a few words of English. It was her first night in this rural part of the country. The landscape seemed all red and yellow, trees were too few and far between to her Midwestern sensibility, and how anyone grew enough food to feed their families was a mystery she would not solve in her brief time with Baba Kapeta, who was both a subsistence farmer and a Shona sculptor.

The day had been long, beginning with the bus ride from Harare to the cooperative, where their arrival was celebrated with music and traditional dance, as well as a communal feast. After the party, students were presented to their new host families. Backpacks were slung over shoulders, and the party dispersed. Americans marched over dusty trails, dependent on these new strangers, to homesteads that were little more than a mud hut or two with conical grass roofs.

Baba Kapeta had a rectangular building of lumber as well as a kitchen hut, some chickens in the yard, his crops, and the outline of an outhouse yet to be constructed. It was this outhouse of the future that made him smile when he showed Anne around her new home. Anne was informed that there were outhouses at the school across the dirt road if she preferred, but that his family went into the brush when they had the need.

During one of their classes at U Zed, a lecturer had mentioned that the word for white person in Shona translates as "people who have no knees," because the first whites to arrive wore pants, hiding their knees from view. She said as a girl, she and her friends would try to spy on the white teachers when they went to the outhouse, because the children found it hard to believe that white people had the same bodily functions as them.

When Anne did make her way across the road to use the outhouse, children were playing in the schoolyard in their ragged maroon uniforms, their skinny arms and dusty legs protruding from the rounds of sleeves and skirts and shorts. Shoes that had become too small had the heels crushed down so they could be worn like slippers. It was boisterous, like any schoolyard anywhere, and Anne wished she had been able to come over when the children were all tucked into their classrooms, watching their teachers at a blackboard. Uncertain what would constitute proper etiquette in this situation and finding herself more strange, more other, here where the language barrier was nearly insurmountable—except when she was with her host father—Anne got in line behind children half her size and waited for a turn in the outhouse. The children around her gasped, exclaimed, and laughed behind their palms, eyes bright with surprise at the inconceivable presence of this *murungu*, with her Scandinavian pink complexion and long blonde braid. Standing in line. With them. For the outhouse.

Here we have the same point of view character in the same broad setting, Zimbabwe, at the same time in her life and in history. The scenario is different. This time, how does Anne feel about this place? Is it familiar? Is it comfortable? How familiar and comfortable does it feel to you, the reader? How much of that has to do with your own experience and how much Anne's perspective?

You can see how the reader is like a stranger in a strange land. Your job as an author is to introduce your reader to your world, and you do that through your point of view character. A story in the world of Zimbabwe is going to be very different if our point of view character is Anne, Amai, or Baba Kapeta. Not only are the three characters' homes, incomes, lifestyles, and education levels very different, but so are their concerns and their world views. You could put them all in the same locale, but you would have three completely different stories because of the differences in their perspectives.

Whichever point of view character you write, you will use that perspective to shape the reader's journey through the story, evoking familiarity, comfort, excitement, their opposites, and any other emotional response that suits the narrative. We saw this in the example above. I kept the same point of view character, but changed the character's experience from comfortable to uncomfortable. Changing the point of view character's response to the world changes the reader's emotional response to the story.

> The point of view character is the reader's vehicle through the story and emotional compass that guides her response to each scenario.

EXERCISE 1: CHANGING WORLDS

In this exercise, you will explore how the point of view character's emotional reaction to a situation shapes the reader's experience of the story.

Note: I recommend you get a notebook or journal and use it for all of the exercises in this book, doing each one as you encounter it. You may already have that notebook from working with *The Story Works Guide* *to Writing Character.* At the end of the process, you'll have created a record of your discoveries about point of view, as well as a manual you can turn to whenever you are exploring how to craft your next story.

This and many exercises involve freewriting. It is a simple practice of timed writing to get things flowing without letting the internal editor get in the way. The rules are: Set a timer for fifteen minutes. Begin writing longhand on paper. Don't stop moving your hand. If you aren't sure what to write, write "I don't know what to write," over and over, until something pops. Then follow that thread. Do not worry about grammar or punctuation. Be sloppy. Be free. Just let words hit the page and keep going. No editing! You'll be surprised by how freely ideas flow when you don't second-guess yourself or bother correcting things.

1. Choose a character you are working with or invent a new one. You will freewrite a scene in which this character enters a new world. He might be a tourist in a foreign land, an orphan being brought home for the first time, a student arriving at college, or a father of three who just moved his family cross-country.

2. Set your timer for fifteen minutes. Ready? Go!

3. Read what you wrote. Answer these questions in your journal:
   - What is the person, tense, number, and distance used in this scene?
   - Is your character entering a world that is comfortable or uncomfortable? Familiar or unfamiliar? Remember,

a scene may be comfortable and unfamiliar or uncomfortable and familiar.

- As a reader, how do you feel about the scene?

4. Now, use the same character and point of view, but send her into a new world. If the first one was comfortable and familiar, make this one uncomfortable and unfamiliar, or vice versa.

5. Set your timer for fifteen minutes. Ready? Go!

6. Read what you wrote. Answer these questions in your journal:

- How does your story change with the shift in scenario?
- How does your experience as a reader change?
- Was it easier to write a comfortable point of view character in a familiar scenario? Or the opposite? How so? Why?
- What did you learn from comparing the two scenes?

RECAP

In this chapter, we discussed the basic elements of point of view. We also considered the way a reader enters a new world upon entering a story. Her experience of that world depends on the perspective of the point of view character.

- Point of view is the narrative constructs, or conceptual elements, through which a reader experiences the story.
- Point of view consists of four basic elements:

- Person: the pronouns used to identify characters;
- Tense: whether the story is told in the past or present tense;
- Number: the number of characters who are given a point of view; and
- Distance: the emotional distance between the narrator and the point of view character and the psychic distance between the reader and the point of view character.

- Every story has both a narrator and a point of view character.
- The narrator is either omniscient or limited.
- The point of view character's perspective is the vehicle that carries a reader through that story.
- Your story's point of view is the first thing a reader encounters. It can be familiar or unfamiliar and comfortable or uncomfortable for the point of view character and, therefore, the reader.
- Exercise 1: Changing Worlds. In this exercise, you explored how the point of view character leads the reader into scenarios that can be comfortable or uncomfortable and familiar or unfamiliar depending on how they are presented through the point of view character's perspective.

Chapter 4

Heart Your Narrator

THE IMPORTANCE OF NARRATIVE

The *narrative* is the textual element of the story that is aware of the reader and ensures the story is told in a rich, engaging manner. That narrative will have a voice of its own, distinct from the point of view character's voice. The narrative voice defines the style of the piece. We can attribute the narrative voice to the narrator. If your narrator is telling the story, your narrative is all the words on the page we can attribute to the narrator. The narrator does. The narrative is.

No story can exist without narrative. When writers try to be *so* true to their point of view character that they choke off their narrator, or try to write a movie-paced story by skimping on the narrative, we end up with manuscripts that read more like scripts than books. They contain pages of dialogue with very little action, setting, emotional subtext, or mood, and they have no voice.

Those things viewers take for granted in film, you as a writer must never take for granted, because they do not magically write themselves onto the page. You may better understand how necessary your narrator and narrative are when we compare film to literature in terms of who is in charge of bringing the various story elements to the audience.

STORY ELEMENT	WHO'S IN CHARGE:	
	IN FILM	IN LITERATURE
Mood, Style, Voice	Director	Author as Narrator
Character Development	Actor	Author as Character
Dialogue	Actor	Author as Character
Costumes	Costume Designer	Author as Narrator
Setting	Set Designer	Author as Narrator
Properties	Props Master	Author as Narrator
Lighting	Light Designer	Author as Narrator
Sound Effects	Sound Designer	Author as Narrator
Action	Director, Cast, Crew	Author as Narrator & Character

Note: Every play or film begins as a script with a writer or writers. I intentionally omitted that stage of the process in order to focus on the end result that the audience consumes. While a script will note the setting generally, or a facet of costume or lighting design critical to the story, the bulk of those choices are left to the people who produce the story for their specific stage and audience.

Notice how much of the writer's creation is attributable to the narrator, seven of the story elements, while the character only gets control of three. Whew. That's a lot of work for narrators!

WHAT YOUR NARRATOR DOES FOR YOU

Sometimes writers are confused by the term narrator. Narrator makes it sound like a person, or another character, has invaded your story. Your *narrator* is the teller of the story and may be the voice of the author, the author's persona, or a character on the page.

Typically, outside of first person narratives, if the narrator is a character on the page, the author is framing the story with a storyteller figure who directly addresses the reader. The reader assumes the role of member of an implied *audience*. The narrator is speaking to the audience, telling the story. Other than the framing, in which the narrator appears on the page, the storyteller and audience are off the stage of the page.

Whether your story has an authorial narrator or a character as narrator, the narrator will provide the narrative.

A novel's narrative should be no less stunning than a play or film if it is to transport readers to another world, make them want to come back for more, get them to fall in love with your characters, and any other goals you have set for your work. Your narrator can do things your characters can't, see things they would never notice, set the mood, establish time and place, provide sound effects, and otherwise make your story as unique as your personal sense of style.

Your point of view character will be busy living the story events as they occur—acting and reacting, getting into and out of trouble, and finding he simply cannot escape the climax. He will not be describing the weather, observing the mannerisms of other characters, providing backstory, and setting mood, among other things. That is the job of the narrator.

> Every story has two voices: the
> narrator's voice and the point
> of view character's voice.

Let's examine some of the things your narrator does for your story that your character cannot.

EXPOSITION

Every story is a fantasy. It is a creation of someone's imagination crafted into a form intended to be shared with an audience. Even if you are writing about your mundane hometown with its boring subdivisions and plain modern architecture, you must build your world. You must create with words a sensory experience of that place and time. And that is the job of *narrative exposition,* to show the reader elements of the story that the character, who is busy acting, cannot or will not show. My dictionary defines exposition as "the act of explaining something, or a public show or exhibition." The word is derived from exposit, which means expound. That is precisely what you do when you write narrative exposition: expound.

> Because you have a narrator, you
> will write narrative exposition.

Some writers are afraid of narrative exposition. Most often, these are writers who have taken a certain piece of advice to heart that is frequently given, but seldom explained fully.

Show, don't tell.

That bit of advice has cast a shadow over narrative exposition. These writers think anything other than dialogue and a bit of movement on the page is telling.

When we talk about *telling,* what we mean is a flat, dull form of narrative that fails to evoke a sensory-rich experience of the story.

> The puppy ran to his mom. She licked him.

Showing uses narrative exposition to provide specific details that stimulate the reader's senses and create an emotional response.

> The puppy loped over the tall grass, tripping over his large,
> soft paws and tumbling, nose in the dirt, to a stop at his

mother's side. She bent her head to nuzzle him, rolling him over with her snout, and licked his face as she welcomed him back to her.

The first passage reads like stage directions, needing a couple of actors to give it life. The second passage uses the narrative voice to show the characters' movement through a specific setting. It illustrates their relationship and feelings toward each other. It also evokes a cheerful mood with the playfulness of the puppy and the affectionate gesture of the mother. And it did all that in two sentences. They are longer than the two sentences in the first passage—showing does require more ink than telling—but they pay with dividends. Telling is forgettable; showing is memorable.

How memorable? When I was in high school, over twenty years ago, I read Edith Wharton's *Ethan Frome*. The book is set in winter. I remember reading Wharton's evocative narrative about the characters sledding. I felt cold, dark, isolated, and sad. I had a visceral experience of the atmosphere. The story enveloped me so I was included in Wharton's world, despite its contrast to the realities of my muggy summertime world.

Narrative exposition is not only for setting. Use exposition for everything that can bring your story to life. If you "tell," your readers will drift away from your story. If you "show," your readers will *feel* your story.

NARRATIVE EXPOSITION ESTABLISHES VOICE

Your narrator has a *voice*. This is the underlying tone of the story that does not change, no matter the setting or point of view. The voice of the piece will make it a cohesive whole, not just a string of related events and characters. Your narrative voice is like a loaf of bread. Your point of view character's perspective is layered on a slice of the bread, like peanut butter. That second point of view character? Her perspective is spread on another slice of bread, like cream cheese. The bread is what unifies the whole. If the loaf is your novel, each slice is a chapter. Why peanut butter and cream cheese? Because your point of view characters' voices should not mush together, as in a "PB&J." You want to hold them up side by side and see how they create distinct and interesting flavors when layered over those unifying slices of narrative voice.

You can think of your voice as your style. Although millions of authors are writing stories in English, we all create different voices through our word choices, the rhythm of our sentences, the way we control syntax, and other minor aspects of our style, like pet words. There are, naturally, times you need to create a voice to suit the story. An author can construct a voice, using a persona specific to each story she writes, changing it from one book to the next. For example, my historical fiction has a different voice than my contemporary fiction, because I create a voice appropriate to the historical period.

You do have a voice and it will evolve as you do. Give yourself room to experiment and play with narrative. Find a voice that fits the story you're writing and your goals as a writer now. Books in a series should have the same narrative voice. Even within a series, however, don't be afraid to evolve. Avoid a drastic shift that will jar your readers, but expect that readers will appreciate growth.

NARRATIVE EXPOSITION CREATES MOOD

Your narrator will set the mood—cheerful, creepy, or anything else. The mood of a story is like the atmosphere of a room, or like when you walk into a restaurant. You don't create the atmosphere. You move through it. The same is true of your character.

If you were a restaurateur, you would make decisions about the atmosphere you want for your establishment. Are you opening an intimate bistro with cozy tables in dimly lit corners? Or are you creating a family-friendly themed restaurant with large tables, colorful art on the walls, and crayons in plastic cups?

Just as you would make choices about the mood of your establishment, you need to make choices about the mood of each scene you write. The character may complement the overall mood. When the character complements the mood, the mood will be the same for the character and the reader. If a storm is brewing, the character will sense it on the page and the reader will sense it off the page.

Alternatively, the character's mood and reader's mood can contrast, and the juxtaposition can be used to heighten the reader's *tension*, feelings of pleasant anxiety while reading. *Juxtaposition* occurs when you place two elements together in a scene that oppose or contrast each other, in order to heighten the desired effect upon the reader.

For example, suppose you have your antagonist whistling a merry tune while tucking an unconscious woman into bed. The character's mood is cheerful. His actions and attitude reflect that. However, if the narrator describes the bed as dirty, the room as underground, then brings our attention to a table laid with surgical implements, it creates an ominous foreshadowing. The juxtaposition of the character's cheerful demeanor and a normally tender act (helping someone into bed) with a creepy setting will heighten the desired effect upon the reader, which in this case is a very creepy mood.

Sometimes a mood changes and the reader notices this shift before the character does. When the reader knows more than the character, tension increases. In this excerpt from *The Murder in Skoghall*, Jess is hosting a party. She's happy, busy, social. The mood is festive.

"Absolutely." Jess put a hand on each of their arms. "Let's talk more tomorrow." She stepped away from Mike and Carrie Cumming, then sidled between Lora and someone she hadn't met yet, a lanky man easily six-three with hands like shovels. "Excuse me," Jess said as she squeezed through. Near the doorway to the kitchen, Dave and Beckett were talking to Miss Jayne Grundi, an older woman who had grown up in the area and moved back after retiring from forty-three years of elementary education. She owned the ice cream parlor and wrote poetry. Although concerned about Tyler, Jess's thoughts stayed with the Cumming's invitation to be a resident writer. It could be the social in she was looking for. She hoped telling Tyler her news would distract him from whatever was going through his mind. "Hey, Jess," Dave called as she passed by. Jess waved and motioned that she'd be back in a minute or two. Dave nodded and turned his attention back to Miss Grundi.

Even with a party in full swing, the kitchen appeared immaculate. Tyler was nowhere to be seen. Maybe he'd stepped outside. There was an exit off the kitchen where he and the waitstaff took their breaks. Jess walked past the stainless steel prep counters and commercial fridges. She didn't notice that the door to the pantry was open until she was upon it. Tyler stood just inside, his shoulders slumped and head bent forward.

Jess stretched out her arm and touched his shoulder. "Ty..."

His hand shot up from his side as his torso rotated toward Jess, the power of the strike coming from his hips and shoulders. Tyler grunted as his fist struck Jess's face....

The mood shifts when Jess enters the kitchen. I do not tell the reader that things are about to change. The setting does that. The strangeness of it being too clean and too empty with a party going on should be mildly unsettling to the reader. Jess is riding the thrill of the party hostess. She's not sensing any danger. The attentive reader will notice the change in the mood before Jess does—the kitchen is too quiet and Tyler's posture is a warning sign. Here, when the reader senses the shift before Jess, it creates tension, because the reader begins expecting something to go awry that Jess does not see coming. And so, for that brief moment, the character's mood is in opposition to the narrative mood. The shift is slight, but it is enough to signal new dramatic action.

It is through the narrative voice that you create mood, showing not only what the character sees and feels, but also more of what is going on around the character, developing atmosphere in the process.

NARRATIVE EXPOSITION ADVANCES THE STORY THROUGH SUMMARY

Summary is a useful tool, so keep it handy. When you need to show the passage of time or distance, or some activity the character must do that is not really story-worthy, use summary. When you need to provide some backstory, maybe reminding readers in book two of things that happened in book one, use summary. Summary gives the reader what she needs to know without slowing the pace of the story.

Suppose you just drove from Minnesota to Texas, and your friend asks how the drive was. You would probably say something like, "Long and dull. It's all highway, so..." That is a summary of around nineteen hours of drive time, probably with a stop at a hotel along the way. The time and the journey still exist, but they are not particularly worthy of the time it would take to expand upon the details. Of course, the ellipsis infers the listener has probably "been there, done that." For a reader I don't know, who may not have driven Interstate 35 from top to bottom, I might write something like this:

She crammed her 1985 Nissan Maxima so full that the rearview mirror only reflected the dull tan of a cardboard box in the back seat. The mini cooler sat in the passenger's foot well, and the seat was jammed so far forward she'd have to pull over and walk around the car to wrangle a can of Mountain Dew from the cooler. The prime real estate of the passenger's seat had been claimed by a terrarium, home to her pet rat, and a battery-powered boom box. She could not make it nineteen hours through who-knew-how-many country radio stations with her car stereo refusing to either play or eject the last tape she put in, David Bowie's *Let's Dance.* Despite all this, she was determined. She made it to Oklahoma City the first day and found a roadside motel where she did not tell the bouffant-haired woman at the desk that she'd be bringing a rat inside for the night.

When she rolled into Austin the next day, she was glad to stretch her legs. She felt not a sense of arrival so much as a sense of beginning.

The difference between the two descriptions of the long drive is the difference between conversational summary and literary summary. When you are in conversation with someone, you know something about each other, can use nonverbal communication to expand meaning, and the other party can always ask questions. In literary summary, I am telling the reader we are not going to worry about those two days on the road, but we are going to acknowledge that they exist in the timeline of the story, and I will maintain the same degree of engagement with that bit of summary as I do with the rest of my story by using my narrative voice to maintain the story's rhythm and style.

THE POV STRANGLEHOLD

I call it "the *POV stranglehold*" when the writer is committed to putting on the page only what the point of view character can see, smell, touch, taste, hear, and infer. When writers attempt to avoid their narrator, prose gets clunky. Readers are left to trip over sentences like, "Josie saw that Mike winced when he bit into the cake she had made him. He appeared to think it was awful." When I see the POV stranglehold, I know the writer is afraid of telling, instead of showing. Ironically, however, this type of writing results in a lot of telling and little showing, because of the lack of narrative. We write narrators to tell our stories. As I discussed in chapter three, "What Is Point of View," our narrators are intermediaries between us—the writers—and the readers. That is very different from trying to write a story without a narrator.

I've heard tales of well-intentioned writing groups who give poor advice, like insisting that if you are writing in a close point of view, the writer must never leave the protagonist's head. They believe if the narrator does more than describe a simple action on the page, it is some kind of point of view slip. When writers abide bad advice, the world of the story becomes myopic.

When you were a kid, did you ever put the cardboard tube from a paper towel roll up to your eye and look through it? The tube contracts your field of vision to a small circle. Reading a story with the POV stranglehold feels like watching a movie through a cardboard tube. If you aren't sure what that's like, give it a try.

EXERCISE 2: FINDING YOUR VOICE

In this exercise, you are going to practice developing your narrative skills and finding your voice.

You will use narrative exposition to create mood, describe setting, and show action. For this freewriting exercise, write in the authorial-omniscient point of view. That means, write as yourself. Do not try to adopt a persona. Do not use a character as narrator. Be the author seated on high, observing the action from afar. You'll be freewriting, so get your journal and pen.

1. Think of a setting. Some possibilities include a kitchen, a campsite, a barn, a penthouse, a sailboat, or a bathroom.

2. Open the scene by describing the setting in rich details. Establish the light, colors, sounds, and smells in this environment. Bring the setting to life and establish a mood before you introduce the character.

3. Bring only one character into the scene. The character is busy doing something. If the setting is outdoors, maybe she chops wood. If it is indoors, maybe she bakes a cake. Show the character's appearance, her physicality as she moves through the setting, and make her mood apparent in her attitude and actions.

4. Create a dramatic shift. Something goes awry or the character experiences an emotional change. Do this without introducing another character.

5. Set a timer for fifteen minutes. Ready? Go!

6. Read your scene. Answer these questions in your journal:

- What is the mood? Peaceful, angry, joyous, ominous?
- Does your character complement or oppose the mood of the scene?
- How would you describe your voice? Does it feel like your natural, true literary voice?
- What was it like to write a scene with only one character? To focus on the narrative instead of on action and dialogue? What did you learn from this exercise?

7. Repeat the exercise. This time, add another character and use dialogue. Practice maintaining a strong narrative voice with multiple characters on the stage of the page.

8. Repeat the exercise every day for a week or until you feel confident in your narrative abilities. Each time, change the setting and bring in a different character.

EXERCISE 3: NARRATIVE VERSUS PERSPECTIVE

It can be difficult to know what is narrative and what is the point of view character's perspective on the page. When a story is well written, the prose moves seamlessly between the two. The best way to get a grasp on the role of narrative is to grab a story and physically mark it up. Copy a few pages from several of the novels on your bookshelves. You'll want a good sample of material to work with, so choose books from different genres. While you're at it, copy out the excerpt from A Stone's Throw in the Special Section after this chapter. You can

find a downloadable copy of the excerpt at www.WordEssential.com/
StoryWorksPOVBonus.

And do not read ahead. *No peeking at the answers.*

1. Get two highlighters or colored pens. With one color, mark all of the narrative in your copy of the passage from *A Stone's Throw.*

2. Mark all of the point of view character's perspective with your other color.

3. The plain text that remains, anything you did not color, will be either dialogue or simple, stage-direction-type action.

4. Look at the excerpt I marked up for you at the end of the Special Section. All of the narrative is in boldface type. The point of view character's perspective is in italics. Compare this to the one you marked up. How do they compare? If there are significant differences, ask yourself why. What can you learn from the comparison?

5. Make some notes in your journal about this exercise.
   - What did you learn by doing this?
   - Did anything surprise you?
   - If you have shifted your understanding of the narrator and narrative, how will you use this knowledge in your own work?

6. Mark up the other pages you copied from books of your choosing, so you can practice understanding the role of the narrator in different genres and with different narrative styles.

RECAP

In this chapter, we explored the role of the narrator and how the narrator, narrative, and point of view character function together in a story.

- The narrator tells the story to the reader. A narrator may be an authorial voice, persona, or character.
- The narrative is the textual element of the story that is aware of the reader and ensures the story is told in a rich, engaging manner.
- Your narrator can do things your characters can't and see things they would never notice.
- Narrative exposition establishes voice, sets the mood, and advances the story through summary.
- The POV stranglehold is when the writer is choking off the narrative in an effort to be true to the point of view character.
- Exercise 2: Finding Your Voice. In this exercise, you developed your authorial voice by working with narrative exposition to create mood, describe setting, and show action.
- Exercise 3: Narrative versus Perspective. In this exercise, you examined excerpts in order to identify narrative and the point of view character's perspective, learning how they work together in story.

Special Section

An Excerpt from Alida Winternheimer's *A Stone's Throw*

In this Special Section, you will find an excerpt that you can copy or download at www.WordEssential.com/StoryWorksPOVBonus.

Use it for exercise three, "Narrative versus Perspective," to help you learn to distinguish between the narrator's and the point of view character's roles in a story.

Grab two highlighters in different colors. As you read the excerpt, mark every line of narrative in one color. Mark every line you can attribute to the point of view character in the other color. Then go back to the exercise to answer the questions.

Simona finished her latté, and then Hannah drove them across Minneapolis to the north end of downtown along the Mississippi. She parked in front of a large building with a limestone front. The stones had been quarried from nearby Nicollet Island. Greek columns supported the half-dome pediment. Inside the frame of the pediment, farmers toiled in relief, scythes and cradles cutting a bountiful field. The figures moved toward the center where a stock of banded sheaves stood ready. The building had housed the grain market at the turn of the century. It was here that farmers, millers, freighters, bankers, and government officials came together to set the practices and prices for the northwest grain trade. Two rows of large windows faced the street. Natural light would have been crucial to the work of inspecting grain samples that came in on freight cars. The building had sat empty and in need of repairs for decades. The city finally partnered with a number of granting agencies to fund a remodel and designate the building as a hub for social services for women and children. A number of agencies would have offices inside, from crisis centers to career counseling. It was an ambitious project, and Hannah was on the board of directors. She was instrumental in convincing the board that they should use a small percentage of the funds to commission a mural on a large wall of the lobby, and then she had convinced Simona to apply for the job.

The women climbed out of the car.

"Why are we here, Hannah?"

"Come inside." Hannah led Simona up the stone steps and under the pediment. The doors were solid wood with cast bronze handles in the shape of sheaves of cut wheat. They were beautiful and they were locked. "Over here." Hannah called Simona down to the far end of the portico where a standard door with a card reader had been installed. She unlocked the door and ushered Simona inside.

The lobby was cold and dusty. A scuffed wood floor of narrow planks had once gleamed under the heavy traffic of commerce. The chandeliers overhead would not be sufficient to light such a vast space, hence the windows, enough to ensure there'd be light even on a cloudy day. To the far left was a blank wall, two stories tall, unbroken by windows or doors. At the right was a long, dark counter shaped like an L. Originally the pit where the bidding on future grain markets took place, it later became a teller's counter when the building was owned by a bank. The frames and etched glass panes of the teller windows remained. Behind the pit, raised several feet off the main floor was an office with windows that looked into the lobby. There a manager could survey his workforce. At the back of the lobby, directly across from the entrance, were two old elevators with brass dials above the doors. The building exuded the regal, masculine air of early twentieth-century construction. It had been built for the commerce of men. Simona thought there was an ironic beauty to its being repurposed to help women and children in need.

"We're thinking of putting a snack counter and coffee bar in the pit," Hannah said. "Wouldn't that be cool? With lots of tables here, then rugs and chairs in conversational groups over there under your mural."

Simona shook her head. "Say that again."

"People can grab a cup of coffee and sit down with a book or friend over there." Hannah gestured toward the blank wall. "We want it to be an inviting space."

"Go back a little further."

Hannah's smile broadened. "Yeah," she said. "Your mural. You got it."

Simona put a hand out and found Hannah's arm, gripped it for support. "I don't believe it. Oh, Hannah…" She covered her mouth with her hand, shook her head, and looked around the lobby again. "It's really mine?"

Hannah nodded.

Simona went to the wall and put her hands on it, glided them across the surface. Apart from a couple of large cracks, it was unmarred—the largest canvas Simona had ever worked with. She leaned into the wall, pressed her cheek against the cool surface and inhaled the dusty damp scent of plaster. She turned to face Hannah, her features spread in a smile of joy, and pressed her back against the wall. "Tell me everything."

"Everyone loved your work," Hannah said. "Really, the mural you did for the hospice was your coup de grace. And Elise Jasper's recommendation was outstanding."

"Really?"

"Of course, I voted against you."

"Naturally."

"I had to abstain—conflict of interest and all that. Simona…"

"Yes?"

"You can peel yourself off the wall now."

Simona came to stand shoulder to shoulder with Hannah, facing the vast expanse of dingy white wall. The nothingness of it thrilled her.

* * *

Simona lost herself when she painted. The world disappeared and she moved without a conscious thought. Words sometimes popped out, words like there, yes, nice. Words that emphasized a stroke of the brush, or approved a color choice. When her head cleared, she knew she was done, either because she was exhausted or the work was finished. A deep breath. A moment for her eyes to readjust, to take in a distance farther than her canvas, to see something other than color. Only then did she step back and look at the whole, to see what it was she had created.

She picked up vermilion with her brush, loading it heavily. The brush hairs touched canvas. The stroke was fat with energy. It left a rich swath of color. Simona worked quickly on the plump figures, each a different vibrant hue. They nestled up together, rubbed thighs and buttocks, sensual, abstract, it was…

The intercom buzzer startled Simona and she quivered. She set the brush on her easel and wiped her hands on a rag as she walked to the intercom.

"Yes?"

"Simona? It's Peter."

The sound of his voice brought gooseflesh all up and down her arms. She stood frozen, her finger poised over the button.

"Simona?"

She buzzed him up and waited, listening for his approach. The elevator arrived, its metal gate clanged open, then nothing. Moments passed. Simona reached for the door just as Peter rapped against it, and she jumped back. He knocked twice more. She looked through her peephole. Peter stood there, his head slightly bowed by the lens of the spyglass. He was rocking back and forth nervously or impatiently. There was nothing to do but open the door. Simona grabbed the handle and slid the steel door aside on its track, a vestige of the building's life as a garment factory and warehouse.

Peter stood before her, the slush on his fine shoes drying into the leather, leaving a crooked salty line around the toe. He had a cantaloupe clasped to his chest in both hands, a bright orange bow tied around it. A lock of hair fell over his eyes. She had the impression of a schoolboy who'd at last found the courage to approach a girl.

Simona laughed and as she laughed, her fear slid away. She took the melon from Peter. "Most men would have gone with flowers," she said, cradling it in her arms.

"Hello, darling." He gave her a quick kiss. "You've got paint on your cheek." He licked his thumb and gently rubbed it away. Simona held her breath until he had finished and held up his thumb, displaying a burnt orange smudge.

Peter pulled the door shut. He removed his overcoat and hung it on her coat rack, which was overburdened by coats, wraps, bags, scarves, even mittens that stood floppily propped on the rack's pegs.

"Shall I cut the melon?" she asked, and carried it into the kitchen area of the studio.

"Not yet."

The excerpt is repeated below with the **narrative in bold** and *point of view character's perspective in italics*. After you complete the exercise, you can compare your version with mine.

Simona finished her latté, and then Hannah drove them across Minneapolis to the north end of downtown along the Mississippi. She parked in front of a large building with a limestone front. The stones had been quarried from nearby Nicollet Island. Greek columns supported the half-dome pediment. Inside the frame of the pediment, farmers toiled in relief, scythes and cradles cutting a bountiful field. The figures moved toward the center where a stock of banded sheaves stood ready. The building had housed the grain market at the turn of the century. It was here that farmers, millers, freighters, bankers, and government officials came together to set the practices and prices for the northwest grain trade. Two rows of large windows faced the street. Natural light would have been crucial to the work of inspecting grain samples that came in on freight cars. The building had sat empty and in need of repairs for decades. The city finally partnered with a number of granting agencies to fund a remodel and designate the building as a hub for social services for women and children. A number of agencies would have offices inside, from crisis centers to career counseling. It was an ambitious project, and Hannah was on the board of directors. She was instrumental in convincing the board that they should use a small percentage of the

funds to commission a mural on a large wall of the lobby, and then she had convinced Simona to apply for the job.

The women climbed out of the car.

"Why are we here, Hannah?"

"Come inside." **Hannah led Simona up the stone steps and under the pediment. The doors were solid wood with cast bronze handles in the shape of sheaves of cut wheat. They were beautiful and they were locked.** "Over here." Hannah called Simona down to the far end of the portico where a standard door with a card reader had been installed. She unlocked the door and ushered Simona inside.

The lobby was cold and dusty. A scuffed wood floor of narrow planks had once gleamed under the heavy traffic of commerce. The chandeliers overhead would not be sufficient to light such a vast space, hence the windows, enough to ensure there'd be light even on a cloudy day. To the far left was a blank wall, two stories tall, unbroken by windows or doors. At the right was a long, dark counter shaped like an L. Originally the pit where the bidding on future grain markets took place, it later became a teller's counter when the building was owned by a bank. The frames and etched glass panes of the teller windows remained. Behind the pit, raised several feet off the main floor was an office with windows that looked into the lobby. There a manager could survey his workforce. At the back of the lobby, directly across from the entrance, were two old elevators with brass dials above the doors. The building exuded the regal, masculine air of early twentieth-century

construction. It had been built for the commerce of men. *Simona thought there was an ironic beauty to its being repurposed to help women and children in need.*

"We're thinking of putting a snack counter and coffee bar in the pit," Hannah said. "Wouldn't that be cool? With lots of tables here, then rugs and chairs in conversational groups over there under your mural."

Simona shook her head. "Say that again."

"People can grab a cup of coffee and sit down with a book or friend over there." Hannah gestured toward the blank wall. "We want it to be an inviting space."

"Go back a little further."

Hannah's smile broadened. "Yeah," she said. "Your mural. You got it."

Simona put a hand out and found Hannah's arm, gripped it for support. "I don't believe it. Oh, Hannah…" She covered her mouth with her hand, shook her head, and looked around the lobby again. "It's really mine?"

Hannah nodded.

Simona went to the wall and put her hands on it, glided them across the surface. **Apart from a couple of large cracks, it was unmarred—the largest canvas Simona had ever worked with.** She leaned into the wall, pressed her cheek against the cool surface and inhaled the dusty damp scent of plaster. She turned to face Hannah, her features spread in a smile of joy, and pressed her back against the wall. "Tell me everything."

"Everyone loved your work," Hannah said. "Really, the mural you did for the hospice was your coup de grace. And Elise Jasper's recommendation was outstanding."

"Really?"

"Of course, I voted against you."

"Naturally."

"I had to abstain—conflict of interest and all that. Simona..."

"Yes?"

"You can peel yourself off the wall now."

Simona came to stand shoulder to shoulder with Hannah, facing the vast expanse of dingy white wall. *The nothingness of it thrilled her.*

* * *

Simona lost herself when she painted. The world disappeared and she moved without a conscious thought. Words sometimes popped out, words like there, yes, nice. Words that emphasized a stroke of the brush, or approved a color choice. When her head cleared, she knew she was done, either because she was exhausted or the work was finished. A deep breath. A moment for her eyes to readjust, to take in a distance farther than her canvas, to see something other than color. Only then did she step back and look at the whole, to see what it was she had created.

She picked up vermilion with her brush, loading it heavily. The brush hairs touched canvas. The stroke was

**fat with energy. It left a rich swath of color. Simona worked
quickly on the plump figures, each a different vibrant hue.
They nestled up together, rubbed thighs and buttocks,
sensual, abstract, it was...**

The intercom buzzer startled Simona and she quivered.
She set the brush on her easel and wiped her hands on a
rag as she walked to the intercom.

"Yes?"

"Simona? It's Peter."

The sound of his voice brought gooseflesh all up and
down her arms. She stood frozen, her finger poised over
the button.

"Simona?"

**She buzzed him up and waited, listening for his approach.
The elevator arrived, its metal gate clanged open, then
nothing. Moments passed. Simona reached for the door
just as Peter rapped against it, and she jumped back. He
knocked twice more. She looked through her peephole.
Peter stood there, his head slightly bowed by the lens of
the spyglass. He was rocking back and forth nervously or
impatiently. There was nothing to do but open the door.
Simona grabbed the handle and slid the steel door aside
on its track, a vestige of the building's life as a garment
factory and warehouse.**

**Peter stood before her, the slush on his fine shoes
drying into the leather, leaving a crooked salty line around
the toe. He had a cantaloupe clasped to his chest in both
hands, a bright orange bow tied around it. A lock of hair**

fell over his eyes. *She had the impression of a schoolboy who'd at last found the courage to approach a girl.*

Simona laughed and, as she laughed, her fear slid away. She took the melon from Peter. "Most men would have gone with flowers," she said, cradling it in her arms.

"Hello, darling." He gave her a quick kiss. "You've got paint on your cheek." He licked his thumb and gently rubbed it away. Simona held her breath until he had finished and held up his thumb, displaying a burnt orange smudge.

Peter pulled the door shut. He removed his overcoat and hung it on her coat rack, **which was overburdened by coats, wraps, bags, scarves, even mittens that stood floppily propped on the rack's pegs.**

"Shall I cut the melon?" she asked, and carried it into the kitchen area of the studio.

"Not yet."

How similar are our marked up copies of this excerpt? They should be nearly identical. Stage directions create a gray zone where the distinction between narrative and not narrative can be unclear. Those lines of text that do nothing more than tell the reader a character moved are found adjacent to lines of dialogue as often as they are found nestled in a paragraph of narrative exposition. Putting those lines in bold typeface when they are part of a narrative section, and leaving them unmarked when they are paired with dialogue is apropos.

For example, how did you mark the following paragraph? Did you decide it consists of narrative, perspective, or stage directions?

She buzzed him up and waited, listening for his approach. The elevator arrived, its metal gate clanged open, then nothing. Moments passed. Simona reached for the door just as Peter rapped against it, and she jumped back. He knocked twice more. She looked through her peephole. Peter stood there, his head slightly bowed by the lens of the spyglass. He was rocking back and forth nervously or impatiently. There was nothing to do but open the door. Simona grabbed the handle and slid the steel door aside on its track...

We could make the case for calling it narrative, because the narrator describes Simona's actions to the reader. We could call it perspective, because Simona is looking at Peter as the narrator describes him. We could also call it stage directions, because the paragraph consists of a series of simple actions that Simona takes. I call it narrative, because the paragraph, while primarily a list of straightforward movements, is rather long for stage directions, and it has some emotional resonance related to those moments of nervous anticipation we've all experienced. But as you can see, there will sometimes be overlap. The best thing you can do is be aware of the possibilities and keep writing.

By identifying the narrative and perspectives in a story's text, you can easily see both the ratio of one to the other and how they flow together to create a story with three-dimensional characters, an engaging plot, and a visual setting.

Chapter 5

Don't Stand So Close to Me

CONTROLLING YOUR DISTANCE

The stronger the emotional connection we have to someone, the more we care about the danger he faces. Readers must have an emotional connection to your point of view character to care about your story, and narrative distance is your tool for shaping that connection.

Distance refers to the sense of distance between the narrator or the reader and both the point of view character and the events of the story. The author manipulates distance to affect how the narrator *tells* the story and how the reader *receives* the story. There are several kinds of distance that work together to create your chosen effects. They are physical, emotional, psychic, and chronological.

PHYSICAL DISTANCE BETWEEN THE NARRATIVE LENS AND THE CHARACTER

The narrative provides a lens through which the reader experiences everything on the page. Think of the lens on a camera on a movie set. This camera is controlled by the director's vision and how he wants to present each scene of the movie to his audience. Your narrative lens is controlled by you, the writer.

In this most physical, almost measurable sense of distance, you can zoom in and out, controlling the frame around the scene. This is an incredibly useful narrative tool.

For example, at the beginning of any scene, especially one in a new setting unfamiliar to the reader, you will want to provide an establishing shot (to borrow the term from filmmaking). That is, you'll need to provide a description of the scene in order to ground your reader in this new place before launching the action.

Alternatively, if you need to show the reader something very specific, zooming in to tighten the frame around that specific part of the set or action will draw the reader's attention exactly where you want it.

In this excerpt from *The Murder in Skoghall,* the characters drive up to a farmhouse and the narrative describes the setting from far away, giving a broad picture, then moves in as the point of view character, Jess, goes up to the house. By the time a man answers the door, the narrative lens is concerned with the specific details Jess is noticing, zooming in on the old man.

> The drive led past a tree break and up to an old clapboard house with a large equipment shed behind it. The shed

appeared in better condition than the house, though neither was faring well. Old farm equipment littered the side yard, rusted derelicts with mean-looking hooks, turbines, and tires as tall as a man. Jess glimpsed a pickup truck that had to be from the 1950s sitting on its axels, a fender lying beside it in the dirt, tucked between a combine and tractor. Tyler climbed out of his truck slowly, surveying the property with suspicion. Jess hopped out and went up to the front door.

She pulled the screen door open and knocked. The house paint had peeled in great dingy scabs, the old boards underneath exposed, rot visible behind the flakes of once-white paint. Jess tried to get a look through the lace curtains that covered the filthy front windows. She was curious how this house compared to hers, if the front room had a mantle as lovely, if the doorknobs were porcelain or had brass faceplates. If the place were abandoned it would be worth stripping. Jess was wondering how one found out about abandoned and condemned buildings when she heard the doorknob turning. She straightened up and put a smile on her face, preparing to meet her antique dealer with optimism and cheer. She couldn't help a glance over her shoulder at Tyler, who finally left the side of his truck.

A bent old man stood inside the doorway with his shirt buttoned up to the collar and the sleeves secured at the cuffs. He held up his wool pants with suspenders. The only sign he was comfortable at home: the plaid slippers on his shuffling feet. His sparse gray hair lay against his head as though he had rubbed too much pomade into it, though more likely, Jess thought, he hadn't washed it in weeks. "Well?"

"Hello," Jess said. Tyler arrived beside her and took hold of her hand. "We saw the signs for antiques. Do you have any we could look at?"

The old man moved his jaw from side to side, considering the request or maybe just preparing his mouth to speak, like exercising a seldom-used hinge. His eyes were surprisingly bright, shining from the folds of a face as weathered as the house. "Take a look in the shed." He gestured weakly toward the yard and smacked his lips together.

EMOTIONAL DISTANCE BETWEEN THE NARRATOR AND THE CHARACTER

You must also choose how close your narrator is going to get to the point of view character and how emotional he will be about the action on the page. We can divide the choices by impersonal or personal and by close or distant.

Impersonal and Distant: An authorial-omniscient narrator, who is impersonal, will maintain a constant distance that is the essence of neutrality. The emotional power of an authorial-omniscient narrator will not come from the narrator per se, but from the point of view characters' experiences and from the reader's own judgments. In the omniscient, we may enter many or all of the characters' perspectives. It is not the narrator's job to choose favorites, but to present the action on the page for the reader, who will then make up her own mind about each characters' motivations and relationships.

Impersonal and Close: A limited, third person narrator can be impersonal in voice, but close in point of view, creating what is commonly referred to as a close third. This point of view creates strong identification between the reader and protagonist. The typical third person narrator is similar to the authorial-omniscient in voice, but readers experience the protagonist's world as though perched on her shoulder. As such, readers are constantly, deeply concerned with her welfare, opinions, and feelings.

Personal and Distant: An essayist-omniscient narrator, one with a persona, might make judgments and express opinions, bringing his influence to bear on the reader's experience of the story. Because he is omniscient, he can enter any character's head at will, and will maintain a position of narrating from on high, above the action.

Personal and Close: A first person narrator, one who is both the protagonist and the narrator, will be the most emotionally invested with the events on the page, have the most to say about them, and have the most bias concerning each turn of events. As a character, she must have a personality that is expressed on the page. As the narrator, she cannot enter other characters' perspectives, but she can express her feelings about the other characters, thereby shaping the reader's opinions. Whether central or peripheral, she must be the protagonist of the story, and so the distance is as close as it can get, because the only separation between the narrator and point of view character is the chronological distance you choose for her.

The table below provides a basic template of your choices and how they define your narrator. Could you create other combinations? Say a limited, third person narrator who is distant and personal? Sure. You would begin with the template for an essayist-omniscient narrator and strip him of his omniscience. His knowledge of the world would be limited to the knowledge available to the point of view character. In shaping your narrator, examine how each combination of the options will affect your story and therefore your reader.

	DISTANT	CLOSE
Impersonal	Authorial-omniscient	Limited third person
Personal	Essayist-omniscient	First person

PSYCHIC DISTANCE BETWEEN THE READER AND THE CHARACTER

The psychic distance between the reader and character will depend on where you place your narrative lens in relation to the action on the page; how impersonal or personal your narrator is; and how emotionally close or distant the narrator feels in relation to the action. Each of those elements combine to shape the reader's experience of psychic distance.

Let's look at some examples and analyze the distance in each.

Distant

A man came out of the church and stood, surveying the cemetery. The church was in bad need of a fresh coat of paint. His wife lay in the small cemetery. Two facts that grieved him daily.

Middle

Reverend Hansen left Gethsemane Church, a small clapboard structure in need of a fresh coat of white paint for some years already. He sighed at the thought of it and headed across the yard to the rectory. He stopped to look out over the small cemetery, his eye drawn as by a magnetic force to his wife's grave.

Close

Reverend Hansen left Gethsemane Church, a small clapboard structure in need of a fresh coat of white paint for some years already. He sighed at the thought of it. *Would the tiny congregation ever be able to afford even that?* He headed across the yard to the rectory and stopped to look out over the cemetery. The oldest in the county, some of the headstones dated from the 1850s and recalled birthplaces in Norway, Sweden, Ireland, and Germany. His wife was buried there, too. He couldn't bear the thought of leaving her, any more than he could imagine a revival of this country church.

In each example, the narrator is an authorial voice, and the point of view is a limited, third person. The pastor would certainly know about the headstones in the cemetery, so that piece of information does not qualify the narrator as omniscient.

In the distant example, the passage feels impersonal. There is the sense of watching from above and waiting for something more to unfold. We are told that he grieves as a simple statement of fact that in itself lacks emotion. As such, we do not feel his grief with him; we observe it from outside his perspective.

In the middle example, the passage becomes personal, but not intimate. We do not enter the reverend's head. But his actions are fully described and more personal. We know he is concerned about the church, because he sighs. And he is looking at his wife's grave, which we can assume is a habit of his. We can infer that he is bereaved. Also, naming our character instantly personalizes him.

In the close example, the passage becomes intimate. We learn contextual details when the age and makeup of the cemetery are revealed. This gives us a sense of the community the Reverend Hansen serves. We enter his thoughts, which reveal that he is worried about the fate of his church. There is the sense it will be closing sooner than later. This is sad on two levels: The age of the cemetery tells us that this community is very old, and the loss of the church will signal the end of an era and a piece of history will be lost. On a personal level, Reverend Hansen will have to move on to a new congregation, leaving his wife in a cemetery that will surely be neglected as the years go by.

How did you feel about Reverend Hansen and his circumstances in each passage? Typically, as the emotional distance decreases, so does the psychic distance between the reader and the character. If you want your readers to feel a greater sense of relationship with and empathy for your character, decrease the emotional distance between your narrator and character by using details that are specific and personal to the character.

The end goal is always for the reader to feel compelled to read on. So why on earth would you ever desire a distant narrative? It depends on the story you are telling and the effect you want it to have on the reader. I discuss this below, but first, let's cover the role of chronological distance in narrative.

CHRONOLOGICAL DISTANCE BETWEEN THE NARRATOR AND THE EVENTS

When your narrator is also a character in your story, as in a first person point of view, you need to factor the chronological distance into your narrative choices. Why? Because time heals all wounds. The greater the chronological distance—the more time has passed—the less raw and emotional the narrator's perspective on those events will be. Your character as narrator is simply not the same as your character as doer. Your narrator is your character *at a different point in time and space.*

CHOOSING THE RIGHT DISTANCE

When you decide what distance to use in your story, look first at your story, then at your point of view character, and then consider how you want the story to affect the reader. A close narrative is certainly the popular choice, the default even, but that does not make it inherently better than a distant narrative. Let's look at how to choose the voice that will best serve your story.

Your narrative distance will create **intimacy** or a lack of intimacy between the reader and character. Generally speaking, intimacy will create a deeper emotional connection that will in turn create a more emotional experience for the reader.

But suppose your point of view character is a stoic man who keeps his emotions locked up tight. He won't let anyone in and feels it a great asset to be ruled by his rational mind. Such a point of view demands emotional distance. We cannot expect the reader to know the protagonist better than he knows himself or to feel through him what he does not feel for himself.

In this case, the emotional distance may let the reader feel more than the character. The reader's feelings will be projected from the reader's psyche onto the character. Pity is one likely emotion for the reader to project onto or feel *toward* the stoic protagonist.

Another emotion you might effect in the reader is frustration. If our distant narrative shows the reader circumstances that could be otherwise, if only the protagonist would open up, then we have put the reader in a privileged position. She will see and know more than the character, thanks to her depth of feeling. An example of this would be if our stoic man found a woman capable of loving him, but because he cannot reveal his heart to her, she leaves him. The reader might be rooting for the protagonist to change in time to find happiness, thus experiencing more emotion than our tragic hero.

> A distant narrative can be a useful means of effecting emotions in the reader that do not exist on the page. Use it when you want the reader to feel toward the character, instead of through the character.

Related to intimacy is reader **empathy**. When your reader empathizes with your character, she puts herself in his shoes, identifying with him. Readers typically enjoy identifying with the point of view character, because they get to experience an emotional journey by living vicariously through the character.

A reader's sense of empathy can be enhanced by a close narrative, drawing the reader into the psyche of the character. A distant narrative, on the other hand, may seem like it is telling, instead of living the story, making the narrative feel reflective or philosophical. This could be just the thing for our stoic man, for example.

Your narrative distance helps create the **mood** of your piece. Suppose instead of a stoic man, you have a taciturn, inhibited, conservative community. Using a distant narrative voice will reflect the impersonal and constricted mood of the community. Suppose within that community is a vivacious young woman, your protagonist. Her joie de vivre will contrast with the mood created by the narrative, just as her freeness will create tension in the restrained community.

Another time to use a distant narrative voice may be when the story is particularly **intense or graphic**. If you are writing a story of terrible abuse or addiction, for instance, a distant narrative can make the story tolerable for your reader. In the case of a particularly harsh scene, you can spare your reader some of the gory details by "zooming out" temporarily.

You must establish one point of view for your story, but within that point of view, there is room to move and play. This freedom of movement is how we create the rhythm of the piece, shaping the characters' experience on the page, and enhancing our readers' emotional experience.

For example, suppose you are writing a close third point of view. As such, the reader experiences the events of the story as though sitting on the protagonist's shoulder, in close emotional identification with the character. To be consistent, the entire narrative must be told in a close third point of view.

However, you want your story to be suitable for teenagers and your grandmother alike. If your protagonist has to experience something unsuitable for your story and your audience, you cannot increase the emotional distance between the narrator and character without breaking your rules. You can, however, increase the physical distance between the narrative lens and the character during that scene. You might use a scene or chapter break to remove us from that piece of action. You could also go so close that the reader enters the character's senses and focuses on something very specific, like the pattern in the wallpaper, instead of on the physical action of the scene. You might get inside her head and spend time with her thoughts, again, avoiding the details of the action on the page that would be too much for your audience.

This applies to both good things, like a sex scene, and bad things, like bodily trauma or incredible loss. Work with the elements of narrative distance to shape the reader's experience of each event in your story, including those you don't want the reader to really experience.

I TOTALLY GET HER...OR NOT!

As you've discovered, how you shape distance and its effects on your narrative will impact your reader's experience of your story. Whatever your story's point of view, you expect the reader to engage with the point of view character, to *not* remain neutral or impassive while reading. This reader engagement can be placed on a spectrum between identification and opposition, or acceptance and rejection of the character.

> You create a relationship between reader and point of view character that can be placed on a spectrum from identification to opposition, which answers the question, to what extent will your reader feel at one with the character?

Let's look at two examples of a close, third person narrative, in which the reader is brought into the point of view character's perspective, and analyze the effect created by the narrative voice.

This short excerpt is from one of my stories, "First Light" in *The Herd* collection. It is a close, third person, present tense, omniscient narrative. Because it is omniscient, and the characters share time and space and a relationship, the narrative fluidly moves between the two characters' perspectives. The psychic distance is close, because the narrative lens is closely identified with the characters' perspectives, as though the narrative camera is perched on their shoulders.

Keith wakes first and watches Suzie sleep. She looks like a child.

Suzie yawns and stretches her arms. Keith smiles at her and covers his mouth to say good morning. She is charmed by his every little courtesy.

It is nearly seven o'clock and he has to milk the cow and feed the animals. They dress and tiptoe downstairs. Keith makes coffee while Suzie makes toast. They eat in near silence at the kitchen table, afraid of waking Mitch and Rey, who were given the hide-a-bed sofa in the living room. Suzie is pulling on her ankle-high boots when Keith shakes his head.

"Those won't do for a farmer." He hands her a pair of his grandmother's work boots from the mat by the back door.

When they come around the side of the house to the front yard, Suzie stops and catches her breath. The sun is coming up across the fields, lighting the barn from the side. The trees that were drained of color the night before are saturated in the dawn's light, and every green leaf appears rimmed in gold. Suzie wishes she had a camera because she does not have an easel. She does not even have a sketchpad and pencils. She determines to remember the moment. She wants to paint it and give it to Keith.

The first four paragraphs of this excerpt are straightforward, showing the characters' movements as they wake and begin their day. We see from their mundane interactions that they are fond of each other. What we can't tell from the excerpt is they are eighteen and twenty years old. Did you get a sense that this is new love? They just spent their first night together. These routine activities are made special by being a first in this relationship. I purposefully kept the language simple and action straightforward, emphasizing the connection between them, letting the world fall away.

Notice how the narrative and points of view are woven together. Transitions should be clear, but not apparent to the reader.

In the final paragraph, the narrative shows us the landscape that stuns Suzie, described in only two sentences. The narrator pauses the action to show the reader a remarkable sight. And then the narrator enters Suzie's head to give the reader Suzie's reaction to the sight. She wants to paint a picture for Keith.

The beauty Suzie notices signifies a momentous turn in the relationship, for Suzie at least. Magic is happening here, and she hopes to capture it with her art, to immortalize it. Furthermore, by showing her intention to give the painting to Keith, we see that she hopes and expects that he shares her feelings. This passage is significant to the story, however simple it may seem. In fact, this golden moment sets up the climax. The point of view provides subtext and nuance. Minor elements of the scene immerse the reader in Suzie's emotional experience of excited contentment. The world is bright and new.

Now let's look at an excerpt from another story in *The Herd*. "Creatures" employs the same point of view, yet the effect is different.

But there is no time to stand around for the working man. Larry peers into the garbage can, expecting nothing, his hand already swinging the lid closed, and stops. There is something inside. He leans into the can far enough for his arm to reach down, his fingers to scrape inches from the bottom. It is enough for him to grab the edge of the curled paper.

It is a catalog, the bottom of several pages stuck together and browned by a spilled Coke. *Anatolia* is scrawled across the cover, "European fashion for girls with flair!" Larry folds the catalog into thirds and tucks it under his coat front as he casually slams the lid of the garbage can. He walks around and climbs into the cab. With the catalog on the seat beside him, Larry finishes his route. He glances at the cover frequently and smells the burnt caramel tang of the cola that soaked its pages. When he stops for his lunch break, he runs into a convenience store and buys himself a Coke. Although he leaves the catalog in the truck, he thinks about it as he eats his egg salad sandwich and sips his pop. He is not far from the house where he found the catalog, and the two women are at the playground, sipping water while their toddlers throw sand into the air and scream.

Published in *Midwestern Gothic*, vol.10.

This excerpt has the same authorial-omniscient narrator as the previous excerpt. The point of view is a close third, with the narrative lens sitting on Larry's shoulder, seeing the world through his perspective. Yet this close third feels different from the other one. How would you describe that difference?

The difference is in effect. In "First Light," I expect the reader to identify with the characters, to "get on board" with them. The psychic distance brings the reader into *identification*. Who doesn't want to experience new love? In "Creatures," I expect this closeness will make the reader cringe. With "Creatures," the psychic distance brings the reader into *opposition*. Who doesn't want to sit with a guy watching toddlers play while thinking about a girls' clothing catalog? How strong that identification or opposition is depends on the story and the individual reader's perspective, hence the spectrum.

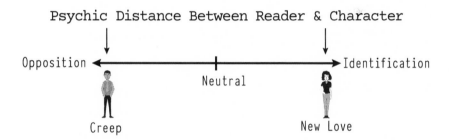

As I've said, the psychic distance is close in both of those excerpts. It is not the distance that creates the effect, but the combination of psychic distance with the character's perspective and actions, as well as the narrative voice.

If I rewrote "Creatures" with an objective narrator and distant point of view, Larry would be far less creepy. He would be a guy eating a sandwich in a park because it's a nice day and he's brown-bagging it. Not creepy at all. What creates the desired and orchestrated reader's reaction is Larry's *fondness* for the girls' catalog, the way he smells the cola and *fetishizes* it, and then, finally, sits in a park eating a sandwich.

In that final, *normal* moment, we don't trust him, because we have gotten close to him and experienced his perspective. Without a close narrative, we would not share his experience of this moment and we would be able to interpret it loosely.

Note: As you just saw in the excerpt from "Creatures," not every protagonist is likable. In fact, any character readers oppose is going to be unlikable or at least uncomfortable. So what keeps a reader engaged? The fascination factor. There are two sides to every coin, and the protagonist must be likable and fascinating. The less likable, the more fascinating. The less fascinating, the more likable. Why would we read about Larry and his girls' clothing catalog? Because we need to find out what he's going to do—that's the fascination factor at play. If you want to learn more about character development, see *The Story Works Guide to Writing Character.*

EXERCISE 4: UNDERSTANDING NARRATIVE DISTANCE

In this exercise, you're going to explore narrative distance, a key element in every point of view. Narrative distance is determined by the narrator's emotional engagement with the action on the page, which then shapes the reader's psychic distance from the point of view character. Distance is determined by the factors discussed above: physical, emotional, psychic, and chronological distance.

You will create your own examples of a close and distant narrative by writing a couple first person scenes.

1. Think of something important that happened to you when you were a kid, at least fifteen years ago. Maybe it's your first crush or the time your best friend betrayed you.

2. Once you've got the incident in mind, put yourself in your own shoes the day it happened. Remember the event vividly and how you felt. Get in touch with those emotions at their full strength. If you were enraged, feel rage. If you were sappy in love, feel sappy in love.

3. Grab your journal and freewrite for fifteen minutes. (If you'd like to review the instructions for freewriting, turn back to exercise one, "Changing Worlds.")

4. Write the incident as you would a scene in a novel with a first person narrator. If you were thirteen at the time, your narrator is thirteen and the experience just happened to him. Let your thirteen-year-old self take control of your pen. Let him pour all of his feelings onto the page. Ready? Go!

5. Read your scene. Answer these questions in your journal:
    - How does it make you feel?
    - Did you relive the experience with emotional intensity?
    - Did you explain the situation on the page?
    - Did you use vivid detail?
    - Did you rationalize or excuse your own or another's behavior?

6. Reset your timer for fifteen minutes and freewrite. This time, write the scene as your mature self, at your current age, looking back on the experience. Ready? Go!

7. Read this scene. Answer these questions in your journal:
    - How does it make you feel?

- Did you relive the experience with emotional intensity?
- Did you explain the situation on the page?
- Did you use vivid detail?
- Did you rationalize or excuse your own or another's behavior?

8. Answer these questions in your journal:
   - Which scene is more powerful? The first one, in which the narrator is your young self for whom the experience is fresh and raw? Or the second one, in which the narrator is your mature self, who has gained distance and perspective?
   - How did each scene affect you as a reader?
   - Which scene was easier to write? Why?
   - What have you learned about narrative distance as a result of doing this exercise?

Clearly, the first passage involves a close narrator, one who is still feeling the effects of the events. The second passage involves a distant narrator, one whose passions have cooled with time and perspective. One who might even be able to account for other people's motives and feelings in this situation.

When you choose to write a close or distant point of view, you are deciding how much of the character's emotional intensity to present to the reader. In our exercise, the character is the same, your young self. The action is the same, that important experience you lived through. But the stories are different because of the emotional distance between the narrator and the point of view character.

Creating chronological distance in a first person point of view is an easy way to see how distance affects narrative, because your narrator has obviously matured over time and gained hindsight. But the same scene could easily be written in the third person. Instead of your mature self as narrator, now use an authorial narrator to provide the sense of distance between narrator, and therefore reader, and the point of view character's emotional intensity. Let's do that now.

EXERCISE 5: THE DISTANCE BETWEEN YOU AND HIM

In this exercise, you're going to further explore narrative distance, this time using a third person point of view.

1. Rewrite the first scene from exercise four. Use a limited, close, third person narrator. You will have the same scenario (perhaps your first crush or the time your best friend betrayed you) and point of view character (that young version of yourself), but now your narrator will be an authorial voice, not a character on the page. Maintain the same emotional intensity of the first scene you wrote. Let your character's perspective on the events dominate the scene.

2. Put yourself in your character's shoes. Imagine the event vividly. Get in touch with emotions at their full strength. Your narrator's emotional distance will be close, so that the reader experiences the event along with your character. Remember that a close emotional distance does not require

a close physical distance; they are separate aspects of distance.

3. Grab your journal and freewrite for fifteen minutes. Ready? Go!

4. Read your scene. Answer these questions in your journal:
   - How does it make you feel?
   - How emotionally engaging is the scene?
   - Did you use vivid detail?
   - Did you relate the experience with emotional intensity?
   - Did you explain the situation on the page?
   - Did you rationalize or excuse any character's behavior?

5. Rewrite the second scene from exercise four. This time, use a limited, distant, third person narrator to present the same scene with the same young point of view character. Your narrator will be an authorial voice whose knowledge of events is limited to what is available to the character. Maintain the same emotional intensity of the second scene you wrote in exercise four (as your mature self looking back). Let your narrator's emotional distance from the events temper the scene.

6. Set your timer for fifteen minutes. Ready? Go!

7. Read your scene. Answer these questions in your journal:
   - How does it make you feel?
   - How emotionally engaging is the scene?
   - Did you use vivid detail?
   - Did you relate the experience with emotional intensity?
   - Did you explain the situation on the page?
   - Did you rationalize or excuse any character's behavior?

8. Now answer these questions in your journal:
    -   Which scene is more powerful?
    -   How did each scene affect you as a reader?
    -   Which scene was easier to write? Why?
    -   Compare the first person scenes to the third person scenes. Write down your thoughts and feelings about their impact on you as a reader and your experience writing them.
    -   What have you learned about narrative distance as a result of doing this exercise?

RECAP

In this chapter, we explored the nuances and impact of narrative distance.

*   By controlling the narrative distance, you influence readers' empathetic connection to the point of view character.
*   Physical distance in narrative exposition functions like the lens on a camera, framing the story for the reader and showing as much or as little of a scene as needed to create tension and advance the story.
*   The emotional distance between the narrator the point of view character is defined as personal or impersonal and close or distant.
*   The psychic distance is the empathetic distance between the reader and the point of view character.

- When using a character as narrator, you must factor in the chronological distance between the time of the events and the time of the telling, because the passage of time affects how much emotional intensity is present in the narrative voice.
- How you shape your narrative distance will affect the reader's sense of intimacy, empathy, and identification with the character.
- Distance helps you create mood and can provide a buffer against intense scenes.
- Successful orchestration of the psychic distance will determine if the reader feels identification with or opposition to the character.
- Exercise 4: Understanding Narrative Distance. In this exercise, you explored narrative distance by writing two scenes in the first person point of view, one close and one distant. The distance was easily shifted from close to distant by changing the narrator's chronological distance from the event.
- Exercise 5: The Distance Between You and Him. In this exercise, you repeated the freewriting of exercise four, but used a third person narrator. Here, you shifted the distance by changing the narrator's emotional distance to the point of view character.

Chapter 6

Making Introductions

THE DOORWAY TO YOUR STORY

Your opening passage establishes your narrative voice and point of view. It introduces readers to the main character, setting, and action. From very few words, readers glean the story you're presenting and quickly make a decision about whether to read on. As readers, we are so used to encountering narrative voice and point of view when we begin reading that we hardly notice it. But as writers, we need to be acutely aware of the narrative and the point of view of every story we write.

Imagine you arrive at a house you have never been to before. You ring the bell. Someone opens the door, and this glimpse through the doorway is your introduction to the world within and its inhabitants. That is what it is like to open a book and read the first paragraph or two. The impression this person and the world inside make will determine whether you enter the house or close the door and move on. Suppose the person opening the door is a sixteen-year-old boy sporting a crew cut and football jersey. Behind him stretches a large foyer with a crystal chandelier over a floor of Italian tile. Behind the boy, a woman in high heels, tight black pants, and a ruffled fuchsia top stands at the bottom of the stairs, one hand holding the banister, the other holding a cocktail.

That fine scenario could open many different stories. What will make this story different, what will draw the reader inside, is the narrative style and point of view.

In those first paragraphs, we need to determine whose story it is, the boy's or the woman's. We need a sense of action: Is the boy leaving the house, the woman watching his exit? We need a sense of the players and their roles and relationships to each other: Is the woman the boy's mother? We need a sense of setting: What time is it? If she's drinking at noon or he's leaving home at midnight, we instantly have a sense of trouble. We need to feel the mood of the piece: Is there a somber tone? A jovial one? Perhaps it's contemplative. Of course, we must know who the point of view character is. Are we in the woman's perspective, watching the boy leave, or are we in the boy's perspective, going forth? And last, the first paragraphs should tell us what the story is about. A family in trouble. More specifically, an affluent family with personal problems, like drinking and strained relationships, a frustrated teenager close to independence, and a mother who has lost control of her family and her life.

You can see from just a few sentences describing the opening scene of a story how much information is set out for the reader. People who are interested in those characters and that conflict will enter the house and get to know the inhabitants and their world. People who aren't interested in those characters or that conflict will go next door, where the door swings open to reveal a sawdust-covered barroom floor. The boy wears leather chaps and a cowboy hat, unwashed hair hangs to his shoulders, and he has dirt under his nails. The woman behind him wears a ruffled skirt over skimpy petticoats and a fuchsia corset over a once-white chemise. She watches the boy as he leaves the saloon, longing for one more chance.

The first sentences you write are packed with information a reader will process without even thinking about it. They establish the voice, style, and tone of the piece, as well as the perspective and mood, which, once established, should not change.

> The wise writer controls his
> story's narrative voice and point
> of view from the first word.

READING LIKE A WRITER

You cannot hope to entice every reader into your story, but you can fairly represent your story as a whole in the opening passage of the book. Doing so will help your book land in the hands of readers who will appreciate it. Let's look at some opening passages and see what we can learn about the narrative and point of view in just a few paragraphs.

After you read each excerpt, pause to think about what you've just learned about the story. Then read my assessment and compare our thoughts.

Here is the opening passage from M.G. Herron's *The Auriga Project.* Find out about M.G. Herron at the back of this book.

Eliana tried her best to look elegant in a black cocktail dress as she drifted across the lawn to greet arriving guests. When her cheeks ached from smiling, and the portion of the quad decorated for the demonstration began to fill up, she adjusted centerpieces and worried the back of one hand with the thumb of the other. Everything had been cross-checked and triple-confirmed: the catering, the press arrangements, the invite-only guest list. Eliana didn't mind the intensive planning required for a big event like this. Organizing and fitting came fairly naturally to a trained archaeologist—she could make sense of that kind of chaos, the kind you could cut and move and change and see.

But all that work was done now. And despite hiring the most capable event planner she could find in Austin, Texas— who at this very moment directed her staff through a wireless microphone like a conductor commanding an orchestra— Eliana fidgeted nervously. How her hands could remain so steady holding ancient fossils yet shake in the presence of her husband's colleagues, she would never understand.

A few pointedly underdressed venture capitalists, several politicians with plastic smiles, and a group of Fisk Industries' brightest minds lounged against the open bar. Above them, a wide screen played clips of rocket launches from the Lunar Terraform Alliance's early missions...

The first word identifies the point of view character, Eliana. This is a close, third person, past tense narrative. This narrator is addressing an audience of readers sympathetic to Eliana, readers who will care about Eliana and whatever is about to happen to her. We can assume this because the tone is pleasantly neutral and Eliana does not do anything objectionable. If the neutral narrator showed Eliana kicking a puppy, we could not be expected to sympathize with her. If the narrator told us that Eliana tried to look her best, but had already spilled on herself, we may be sympathetic toward her, but that sympathy would be tinged with humor, pity, or disgust, depending on the tone of the narrative. We see that Eliana is somewhat uncomfortable, "trying" to look elegant. We learn that she is an educated, professional woman, an archeologist, so we can deduce that she is simply out of her element. This is confirmed in the brief second paragraph, in which she wonders at her nerves around her husband's colleagues. We know that the stakes are high. Eliana is somehow responsible for this event, organizing and hosting it, and it's a role she doesn't fill naturally, which creates mild tension. The reader suspects within the first paragraph that something will go wrong, despite Eliana's triple-checking the details. We can tell from the narrative style that this is a drama, not a comedy, and that we are in our modern world with modern concerns. In the third paragraph, we get a sense of those concerns and the event's importance. Eliana is not only hosting a party critical to her husband's business, but to a space mission that concerns investors, politicians, and rocket scientists.

From this opening, we already know quite a lot about what kind of story this will be and what kind of character Eliana is.

Here is the opening passage from Judy K. Walker's *The Perils of Panacea*. Find out about Judy K. Walker at the back of this book.

The three basic rules of private investigation, imparted to me early and often by my mentor Ralph, are as follows: First, don't work for free, no matter how good the cause. Even the most appreciative client will eventually succumb to human nature and think he's getting exactly what he's paid for. Second, don't work for family or friends. That's pretty self-explanatory, at least to anyone who has family or friends. Third, don't work for anyone you really don't like. Come to think of it, if you really don't like someone, you probably know that person well enough that he or she should fall under rule number two.

Strictly speaking, all of Ralph's rules can be reduced to one rule applicable to both investigation and life in general. I've taped it, typed in twenty-eight point font all-caps, to my desk at the office and above my computer at home, and I probably should put it next to my bed. (Then again, I should be so lucky as to need it there.) I refer to it as Ralph's Law: "DON'T BE A DUMBASS."

The first sentence here establishes a first person, past tense narrative. We can tell that the person telling the story is a central narrator, but we do not know whether this narrator is male or female, young or old. We do know he or she is old enough to no longer be under the wings of a mentor named Ralph. That first sentence is formal in tone, but we know by the second sentence that this narrator has a sarcastic sense of humor. The more we read, the more this is confirmed. The narrator has a conversational approach to storytelling and does not take him or herself too seriously. The narrative voice is not chummy enough to say the reader is a personal friend, but the reader is certainly sympathetic to not only the narrator's perspective, but to the character and the trouble that seems to follow him or her around.

Do you think this character is a male or female? Why? What about the narrative voice makes you think that?

We learn in the first sentence that *she's* a private investigator. We figure out from the discussion that she's not much of a rule follower, even when she tries, even when the rule is handed down from on high. The tension in this opening passage is created by the allusion to breaking Ralph's Law. We know that as a result of that breach, this character is about to get into trouble.

This opening passage establishes the first person narrator's distance. The narrator has lived to tell the tale, so we know the events occurred in the past relative to the telling. The distance, however, is not great. She's not rocking on the porch of the old folks' home. Maybe she's perched on a barstool with some fresh bruises from the ordeal. We get the sense that things are recent enough she might still feel bad about them, like maybe she was a dumbass. She might have learned her lesson, but there's probably more to come. The story, then, is in the recent past, both chronologically and emotionally.

Whereas Herron's opening did not reveal much about the scenario—it's an important party and *something* is about to happen to Eliana—we know from this first person narrative that the private investigator took a case she shouldn't have. It is her mistake and she is going to pay for it. Herron is using a close, third person narrator who is limited to the point of view character's knowledge base. Eliana does not know what's about to go wrong—she's focused on not tripping in her high heels—and neither do we. We only know it's *something* because of the tension. Walker's narrator, however, knows exactly what will happen—she has lived it already—and is giving us a clue in the opening passage: *mea culpa*. Herron's close, third person narrator does not reveal things the point of view character cannot know. Walker's first person narrator has access to the time and events that are behind her. She knows more than the character in the moment, but not more than herself at the time she tells the story.

Both passages do their jobs well: introduce and *hook*.

Here is the opening passage from Aldus Baker's *Hidden Ability*. Find out about Aldus Baker at the back of this book.

Scrub oak and evergreens gave way to brush and grass where Krenis dismounted and rushed to the overlook. As he had feared, the carriage had heedlessly entered the narrow way and been forced to a halt by a barricade of logs and stones. Arrows rained down on the carriage. The driver struggled to back the horses away from the barrier in a worthy attempt to escape the trap. An arrow struck the driver's right arm. The man howled in pain and shouted curses at his frightened and confused team.

The bowman had abandoned his seat next to the carriage driver. He appeared to be using the horses and carriage to shield him from the enemy archers. Krenis spotted two of them on the far hillside. The sound of a bow gave away a third archer on the slope below him.

The passage opens *in media res,* in the middle of action, with life-or-death stakes. Arrows are being fired on a trapped carriage. The point of view character is Krenis, a rider witnessing an attack. We know immediately that he is on the side of the people with the carriage, which is established at the beginning of the second sentence, "As he had feared." The distant, third person narrative voice is concerned with establishing dramatic action. We are not inside Krenis's gut, feeling his adrenaline spike. Instead, we are peering down on him, taking in the scene while he sizes up the situation and prepares to enter the fray.

The emotional distance in Baker's opening creates the effect that readers do not worry about Krenis personally. We sense that the stakes are all about the people inside the carriage. Krenis has a duty to fulfill, and if he dies, we will not mourn him, but the failure of that duty. Whereas in reading Herron's opening, we focus on Eliana and her experience of this big event. We know whatever is about to happen, it will turn her life upside down. In the former, the narrative distance (distant) puts the focus on the scenario. In the latter, the narrative distance (close) puts the focus on the character. While in Walker's first person narrative, we know that whatever rotten thing happens to the narrator, she manages to survive it, and so whatever we feel for her while she's in danger, we are assured of the outcome.

Baker's narrative voice establishes the setting as the distant past, a time of carriages and arrows. We may not be certain whether this is a Wild West or a medieval story from these paragraphs, but the words *bowman* and *enemy archers* are probably enough to put us in the right vicinity. The narrator is addressing an audience of readers that is after action, adventure, and a hero. This opening is all about setting up the fight, an exciting introduction to a world of conflict. Contrast that to Walker's opening passage. Being a detective story, we can expect action and danger, but the opening passage establishes that the story is character-driven, while Baker's story is action-driven—as far as we can tell from this passage.

Note that Baker's story opens with a prologue; although Krenis is the point of view character in this passage, he is not the main character. Because of the narrative distance in this opening, we don't get too attached to him. It is a useful example of how narrative distance affects the reader's connection to a character.

Let's look at the differences between these three opening passages again, side by side.

	HERRON: THE AURIGA PROJECT	WALKER: THE PERILS OF PANACEA	BAKER: HIDDEN ABILITY
Point of View	Close, third person, past tense.	First person, past tense.	Distant, third person, past tense.
Narrator	Authorial voice, limited, neutral.	Close chronological distance, informal, has a sense of humor.	Authorial voice, limited, neutral.
Audience	Assumed sympathetic to the protagonist, interested in a character who is out of her element.	Assumed sympathetic to the protagonist, interested in solving crimes.	Assumed to enjoy action and adventure in the distant past.

Emotional Distance	Close with a focus on Eliana's experience of the event and concern about her welfare.	Close with a focus on the promise of a tale to be told, since the character's welfare is known before the story begins: she lives to tell the tale.	Distant with a focus on the event, instead of the point of view character, with concern over the event's outcome instead of the character's welfare.
Source of Tension	The protagonist is uncomfortable at a big, important event that has to do with her husband's career.	Narrator reveals that she has made a mistake, broken Ralph's law.	Story opens with an attack on unknown victims.
Clues to Genre	Drama, technology, near-future setting, rocket launches and "Lunar Terraform Alliance."	"Private investigation," tone of narrative voice.	Bows and arrows, life or death action.

The first sentences you write in any story establish the point of view and provide the reader with a large amount of information about what's to come. This information helps the reader assess whether or not to keep reading. Your reader may only be aware of this on an instinctual level, but as an author, you need to be aware of the choices you're making so that you can control how your story is introduced to your reader.

Note: The only thing that may not be established in the opening passage is whether a story has multiple points of view. Introducing several points of view in a single paragraph or two would be jarring to readers.

EXERCISE 6: OPENINGS AND WHAT THEY TELL US

In this exercise, you're going to assess the opening paragraphs of a variety of stories. You will learn to identify point of view and narrative distance and analyze how the choices the author made affect you as a reader. Use these elements of point of view listed in chapter three: person, tense, and distance. We can assume that in the opening paragraphs you will only meet one point of view character, so number will be moot for this exercise. You should, however, be able to tell if the narrator is limited or omniscient.

1. Grab some books off your shelves. At least ten. Make sure you get a variety of genres. You can also go online and work with the sample pages of books, which might be fun since you can choose books you have never read. When you open those samples, make sure you're reading the first paragraph on the first page, be that prologue or chapter one.

2. After you read the opening passage of a book, open your journal and write down the title and author. Then identify the point of view person, tense, and distance. If the distance is distant, check whether you read a prologue (as in Baker's

Hidden Ability example above) or the first chapter. Is the point of view limited or omniscient?

3.   Having identified the point of view and narrative distance, examine how you felt reading the opening passage. Write down your reaction to it as a reader. There is no right or wrong; there is only your subjective experience of the author's choices. Answer these questions in your journal:

    –   Is the point of view comfortable for you?
    –   Is it similar to what you like to write?
    –   What can you learn from this exercise?
    –   Is there something you would like to try in your own writing? Or something you would like to avoid in your own writing? Take a minute to write down why that is.

4.   Look at your answers to question three. As the writer, you can craft your story to create a certain experience for your reader. That's why whenever you read something, you should pause to ask how it affected you. Then ask why. Then ask if it is something you would like to replicate or avoid in your own work.

CONTROL FREAKS WELCOME

Readers make snap judgments about whether or not to bother with a book. You might have a book for sale that's not moving, but the few people who have read it love it. You think, *if only people would give it a chance!*

It is your job to make sure the only chance readers need to take is right there in that opening passage. You do not need everyone to love your book, but you do need the readers who would love your book to walk through the front door. A hook compels the reader to swing the door wide open. Your narrative voice and point of view invite them in to get comfortable.

Establishing a story's point of view and narrative is inevitable. Controlling it is the next stage in your evolution as a writer.

RECAP

In this chapter, we looked at opening passages and how they quickly establish the point of view and narrative voice of any story.

- Opening a book is like opening the door on a house you've never entered before. What you glimpse inside will determine whether you cross the threshold or go next door.
- Besides hooking your reader with some compelling action or emotional movement, your opening passage will establish your story's narrative style and the point of view.
- The only aspect of point of view that a reader may not determine in the opening passage is whether a story has multiple point of view characters.
- Exercise 6: Openings and What They Tell Us. In this exercise, you looked at several opening passages from various stories and analyzed the point of view. You also examined the effect it had on you as a reader.

- Controlling point of view in your opening passage could be the difference between your book finding lots of readers and your book finding those patient few who get through the front door.

Chapter 7

The Right Point of View

EENY MEENY MINEY—NO

Your story's point of view should be a conscious choice you make as a literary artist. It should be earned by you and any characters you crown with the designation of "POV." Even when a point of view just feels right, you should be able to describe why it is the best point of view for the story. If you can't explain why *this* story is best told in *this* point of view, the point of view is not earned.

WHY CHOOSE ONE POINT OF VIEW OVER ANOTHER?

Which point of view you choose depends on your goals for the story. These goals relate to

- craft and the story's structure,
- audience and the effect you want the point of view to have on the reader, and
- creative process and artistry.

All of those reasons are valid, and you might have other reasons of your own. Just remember the cardinal rule:

> You can do anything you want, so long as you do it well.

HOW TO CHOOSE YOUR POINT OF VIEW

As you decide which point of view to write in, consider the factors listed above: craft, audience, and artistic goals. The best choices will often seem organic to your story, suggesting themselves to you. But you are wise to weigh any possible choice against another. Sometimes the options that suggest themselves do so not because they are organic to the story, or best for it, but because they are the most comfortable to the writer.

Let's look at some examples to illustrate how these factors come together when choosing your story's point of view.

In The Skoghall Mystery Series, I chose to write in close, multiple third, past tense. That means I maintain a close narrative distance, have multiple point of view characters, and I am telling the story in the third person and past tense. The designation "close" means that my narrator is concerned with the characters' experiences and perspectives in the *now*-story and my narrator is limited to the knowledge available to my point of view characters at the time of the story. Because of the roles of the chosen point of view characters, these parameters actually afford me a great deal of freedom.

Remember, if the narrative is not designated as omniscient, limited is safely assumed. Also, limiting the narrator to the information available to the point of view character still gives you plenty of room to notice and report things the character doesn't, won't, or can't in that moment. The shadow on the floor? The character would never notice it, but the narrator does. Why? Because it has a desired effect, such as creating mood or foreshadowing trouble. If the character is lying on the floor, unconscious, there is nothing he can report to the audience. But the narrative lens, which creates the audience's window on the action, can show the entire scene: the character, the unmade bed against the wall, the setting sun outside the window, the sound of a car arriving in the drive, the owl landing in the tree behind the house.

> The narrator's job is to show
> the reader the stage of the page
> and everything in the scene.

Within the series, the world consists of Skoghall and the surrounding area. Within that world, my protagonist, Jess, is surrounded by a set of supporting characters. They are the continuing cast of Skoghall. And in each book is a killer, or killers, and a victim. They are transient, existing only in a single book. Within the relatively constant members of the community, I like to think of The Skoghall Mystery Series as a single, close, third person narrative, because only my protagonist, Jess, gets a point of view. But within the transient cast of a single book, I give my antagonist and my victim points of view. Their chapters tend to be short asides that enhance the main story.

Why did I choose to add these transient point of view characters to my series? My reasons relate to craft, audience, and artistry.

Craft: I could have written a standalone prologue in the killer's perspective and never entered the killer's head again. Prologues let you do that by standing separate from the rest of the story. But I liked the idea of periodically visiting the killer's perspective to show his trajectory through the story.

Audience: I crafted these perspectives with certain effects in mind. When I wrote the antagonist's scenes, I focused on increasing dramatic tension by showing how scary and troubled this person is. When I wrote the victim's scenes, I increased empathy by showing the character as more than a ghost, as someone you might really like, who had a life and loved ones before becoming the victim.

Artistry: I examined stories from multiple angles and wrote stories within stories. It was not enough for me to know the bad guy would be caught at the end. I wanted to know why the bad guy is *bad*.

When I wrote *A Stone's Throw,* I chose a close, multiple third, past tense point of view.

Craft: The story focuses on two women's evolution as a result of an affair. The story is about a love triangle, so it felt natural to have three point of view characters. Using three point of view characters makes plain that all of my characters are right and wrong, that they all have loved and wronged each other. If I had written only in the wife's perspective, it would have been a story about a woman wronged. If I had written only in the lover's perspective, it would have been a story about illicit love. And if I had written only in the man's perspective, it would have been a story about the conflict between duty and desire.

Peter is a primary character with a point of view, but he is not one of the protagonists, so he does not receive equal time.

Audience: I wanted to effect empathy for all three of my characters and to ensure Peter came through as a flawed but likable human. Why did I give him a point of view at all? Because I wanted Peter to have a voice. His motivation for and perspective on these relationships matter. To me, he is likable, sensitive, and loving. He is in a difficult situation and makes choices that have both good and bad repercussions. Just like the women. If he did not have a voice, he might seem cliché—the philandering male—seen only through the eyes of the female characters. I have heard from readers that they detested Peter at the beginning of the book for having an affair. But as they read on, they came to like him. This confirms what I suspected, that by giving Peter a voice, readers are able to see him as a real person with virtues, as well as flaws. Giving him a point of view means readers could not see him as a scapegoat.

Artistry: I wanted to explore the themes of the work with a narrative fluidity that created shifting allegiances between the characters themselves and between the reader and the characters. I also wanted to contrast Simona's journey with Gemma's.

I developed my characters' arcs so that Simona and Gemma are on parallel journeys, but their trajectories cross in the middle. Late Simona mirrors early Gemma. I had to show, through the women's perspectives, their personal evolution. They are both on journeys of self-discovery, but as Simona loses herself, Gemma finds herself. I picture their arcs not like this:

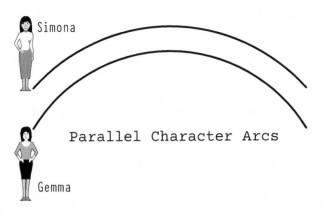

Parallel Character Arcs

But like this:

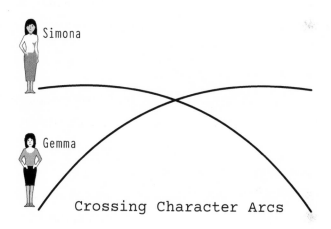

Crossing Character Arcs

Did I succeed? I believe I accomplished what I set out to do artistically. Supporting this belief, I have heard from readers that they like Simona best at the beginning of the book and Gemma best at the end.

Note: When I say "I've heard from readers," it is because I've arranged author events at community centers and with book clubs. Author events allow you to glean information you won't typically find in online reviews. I recommend writers connect with readers to discuss the written work whenever possible. It's illuminating and rewarding...and you just might find yourself saying, "I've heard from readers..."

EXERCISE 7: MAKING THE RIGHT CHOICE

Is there really a right and a wrong point of view for a story? There is certainly a best point of view for each story. Take out your journal. Instead of freewriting, you'll be reflecting.

1. Think of the story you're beginning or the one you plan to write next.

2. Answer these questions in your journal.
   - What point of view are you using or planning to use? Consider person, tense, number, and distance.
   - How will this point of view help you more effectively **craft** your story?
   - How will this point of view affect the **audience**?
   - What are your **artistic** goals with this story? How will this point of view help you accomplish them?
   - How many point of view characters are you planning to use?
     o Make a list of them and justify each one.
     o If you do not have sound reasons to include all of them, cut the dead weight.
   - How would this story change if you switched to another point of view?
     o Select two or three variations and reflect on how those changes would affect the story, the audience, and your artistic goals. For example, from a close third to a distant authorial-omniscient. Or from a

      multiple third to a first person. Changing even one element of your point of view can create profound changes to your story.

–   Have you affirmed your original choice, or did you discover new possibilities? Reflect on what you have discovered about choosing the best point of view, generally, and for this story, specifically.

You now have a better understanding of how to choose from the various elements that together craft your point of view. In the next four chapters, we'll sharpen that understanding by discussing specific points of view in depth. We're starting with everybody's friend, the third person narrator. Then we'll spend some time partying with multiple perspectives. Next up, shine your shoes and smooth down that cowlick for the most powerful, the all-seeing, all-knowing omniscient narrator. Then we'll get personal with the first person narrator. After all that, we kick off the special topics chapters by entering the den of the unreliable narrator, so grab your lie detector kit!

RECAP

In this chapter, we looked at the considerations that go into choosing your point of view and how that will impact both your story *and* your reader's experience of your story.

- The point of view you choose will shape your story's structure.

- Your choice of point of view depends on the best way to craft the story, the effect you want it to have on the audience, and your goals as a literary artist.
- Exercise 7: Making the Right Choice. In this exercise, you reflected on how to best craft the point of view for your story. You also considered how other possibilities could change the story.

Chapter 8

He Said, She Said

THIRD PERSON IS NOT JUST HEARSAY

The third person is familiar and comfortable for any reader in any genre, so it is comfortable for most writers to begin a narrative in the third person, even if he doesn't understand why.

It is simpler to write in the third person than the first person point of view, and the reason is because the character and narrator are separate entities. There is no confusion over who is telling and who is doing. The narrator still gets to enter the character's head and report what he is thinking, feeling, and wanting. The narrator can also, significantly, give us history, backstory, and explore things the character could never know or would never notice.

In the literature of past centuries, authorial-omniscient was the point of view of choice. In modern literature, a close, third person point of view is prevalent. I consider a close, third person, past tense, singular point of view to be the default for contemporary literature. Third is currently the point of view that needs no justification. An author could ask, so why *not* write in third person?

> The third person point of view is the most commonly used and is in many ways the easiest to write.

THE NARRATOR AS GOD, OR IF YOU PREFER...ANTHROPOLOGIST

Once you have decided to write a third person point of view, the next question becomes, omniscient or limited? I'll discuss the choice here and will go into depth about the omniscient point of view in chapter ten, "Playing God."

The classic authorial-omniscient narrator mimics the role of God and refers to characters in the third person. The narrator assumes a position of privilege with readers, that of God over the world created on the page. This is not an Old Testament God, burning bushes and smiting sinners, but a New Testament God who sits on high and watches all, allowing free will to determine the fates of those he observes. For literary purposes, however, God's primary role is not observing, but storytelling. What makes her godlike is the ability to enter the mind and heart of any character. More importantly, she is not bound by time and space.

Very few people are writing authorial-omniscient narratives these days. In *The Art of Fiction,* John Gardner suggests any writer who wants to do so, "needs only to imitate, say, Tolstoy" (159). Although some of them may very much admire Tolstoy, I have yet to meet a writer who professes that he wants to imitate Tolstoy.

With the proliferation of multiple, close, third person narratives, you may ask what the difference is between a multiple third point of view and an omniscient narrative? Especially when some of the current genre-bending books have *many* point of view characters. And often *too* many. The difference of greatest concern between a multiple, limited, third person and an omniscient point of view is that the omniscient narrator is *omniscient,* not limited, in her scope of knowledge. I'll discuss the nuances of this distinction in chapter nine, "Keeping Them All Straight" and chapter ten, "Playing God." Now, let's dig into an updated analogy that might suit you and your limited, third person narratives well.

Time to come down from the clouds and put on your best pith helmet and khaki dungarees.

THE POWER OF OBSERVATION

I majored in anthropology as an undergraduate. In the early days of anthropological study, anthropologists remained above and beyond the cultures they studied. They entered remote areas and introduced themselves—white, Western, professionally dispassionate social scientists—to the culture. They hoped they would not influence the community through their mere presence. One of the pioneers of the field was Margaret Mead. I have an image of her, inspired by a professor's offhand remark, of a middle-aged white American woman sitting on the whitewashed porch of her bungalow in Papua New Guinea, watching the lives of the villagers from a careful distance. This image, however inaccurate, has been burned into my imagination.

Turns out, the image is useful, because the third person point of view narrator is just like Margaret Mead, sitting a careful distance from the action, observing and reporting all to a specific and known audience. This narrator is invisible to the characters. She has no influence on events whatsoever, but she describes them for her readers. She is not a mere reporter, however. She is a cultural anthropologist. An analyst. A philosopher. A psychologist. Above all, she is a bard.

Say our imaginary anthropologist returned from months in the field to tell her colleagues that the people in the imaginary village of Misetemia ate plantains every day and had an average of four children per family. She would be kicked out of the ivory tower of academia. There is more to understanding a culture than taking a head count and recording dietary preferences. That *is* part of it, but only a tiny fraction.

Our anthropologist must consider the big picture, such as climate, topography, and seasonal changes that affect people's lives. She must observe physical artifacts, like dress, buildings, manners, rituals, music, and other art forms. She must try to understand the intangible aspects of life, like beliefs, customs, humor, grief, and relationship structures within this society. The knowledge and understanding she gains must be woven into a narrative that is carefully crafted so that her readers can develop a picture of this "other" culture based upon her field work. Her goal, far removed from any colonial ideology, is to increase our understanding of humanity.

Your job as a writer is to develop a narrator who is like the anthropologist. She writes her story to increase her readers' understanding of what it means to be human. She must account for the world picture, the physical artifacts, and the intangible aspects of life while weaving all of her carefully selected details into prose capable of not only fascinating an audience, but also of moving them.

Your anthropologist narrator is no more omniscient than our pioneering scientist, Margaret Mead. The narrator only knows what she can know, which is more than the characters, but less than God. She knows more than the characters because she is a trained observer watching all from the perfect vantage point—her whitewashed porch. She is astute, careful, and particular. She observes the sunrise over the hills, notes the crow of the cockerel, knows exactly which person rose from bed first, and saw who forgot to wash behind his ears. All of this may be amazing, but it is not superhuman.

Now, when you are deciding whether to write in the omniscient or the limited, third person point of view and need a quick and easy way to frame the question, simply ask:

Is my narrator God? Or Margaret Mead?

PSYCHIC DISTANCE IN THIRD PERSON NARRATIVES

It may seem that using third person pronouns will make the reader feel a greater degree of separation than if the prose were written in the first person. In practice, however, it all depends on execution. Psychic closeness is not all about the point of view character. It is also about the narrative voice. A reader may very well feel more engaged with a third person point of view character than a first, if the story is told to effect closeness.

Third person creates, by virtue of the pronouns used (he, she, and they), a separation between the narrative voice and characters. This separation can help the writer find the most effective narrative voice, one that is distinct from the point of view character. Also, because of this separation, the narrator becomes invisible to the reader. She is ever-present, like background music, shaping the reader's experience without the reader necessarily being aware of her.

If you have ever seen a movie scene that's had the soundtrack removed, you know background music plays a large role in the emotive power of a scene, heightening the dramatic effect of any moment, any emotion. Your narrative voice, the music of your prose, has that same power. The words on the page create the story the reader sees in his mind's eye: the actors, the action, the dialogue, the setting. But your careful choice of every syllable, the way the words sound and act together, their tempo and mood, create an emotional response in the reader.

FOREVER CHANGED

No matter what point of view you write in, the protagonist of the tale should be forever changed by the events of your story. That is what the *character arc* is all about. If you have any doubt about developing a character arc, read this book's companion book, *The Story Works*

Guide to Writing Character. A single, close, third person point of view is so much like a first person point of view that in both "point of view character" and "protagonist" are synonyms.

GETTING CLOSE

In this excerpt, we have a single, close, limited, third person point of view. Notice how similar the close, third person is to the first person point of view. Though most of this passage is narrative, the narrator is so intimately engaged with Marla's perspective that we feel as though we are experiencing the world *through* her and not only *with* her. Notice how the narrative reflects Marla's attitude toward her situation, creating a close psychic distance between the reader and character.

June had cried all day. A grown woman of fifty and unable to check her emotions. She cried that morning while helping fix Marla's hair, and Marla had held her. She cried in the church during the service, and Marla had patted her knee. At the graveside, June began dabbing at her nose with a tissue, and Marla simply stared at the coffin. She would tell June she wanted to be cremated later, in a month...or two.

June had been the last to leave, insisting the house would be too quiet. Marla replied it would be fine. She couldn't bring herself to tell June to go away and leave her alone. She undid the last button and let her black dress drop to the floor. It lay in a soft heap ringing her feet. She stepped out of it and started to bend. She stopped, straightened up, and kicked it to the side. She stood in her under-things—modest in a full slip. Rayon. She'd never bought silk because it seemed too fine a thing for her life.

Having a daughter meant that Marla went without. Year round she saved. As long as Tom never saw a bill, June could have the things Marla wanted for her: ballet lessons and summer camp, braces and a prom dress. Each time she took her allotted fifty dollars to the grocery store, her purse bursting with coupons, she came home with at least ten dollars to hide away.

She scooped out cold cream with her three middle fingers and rubbed at her softly fallen cheeks. It struck her how still the house was. Normally at that time of day, Tom was laid out behind her, snoring while the ten o'clock news blared over the television. He woke up each time she turned the volume down and complained, "Hey, I was watching that. I need to see the weather, you know."

"You old fool," she said aloud and blotted away cold cream with a tissue. "You never went outside the last three years. What did you care about the weather?"

GETTING TOO CLOSE

The POV stranglehold is a common problem with the limited, close, third person point of view. It becomes especially pronounced when writers are afraid to step out of their character's perspective and use precious ink writing out every detail of the character's day.

Being true to your point of view character does not require taking the reader on a forced march through every slogging step of the character's journey.

When writers provide readers with too much of the character's daily grind, the story becomes hyper-real. This issue can go on for entire chapters, because most, if not all, novels contain a traveling chapter or several. Those are the times when the protagonist has to get from A to B. That might be the detective doing some legwork or the adventurer crossing the desert. Whether mental or physical, traveling chapters get dull for the reader. Whatever rules you establish for the world you've built, your character must abide by them. Gravity? Linear time? A body that needs time to heal wounds? Or flight? Time travel? Magic potions? No matter how powerful your character, your narrator is more powerful. He's the one who can stand outside the rules of your world to shape the reader's experience. Need to fold time to minimize the traveling chapter doldrums? No problem.

Writing the hyper-real denies your narrator use of his super powers and does the reader a disservice, making her sit through the character's actions when those actions do not advance the story's plot, character, or theme. By keeping that always in mind, you'll be able to carefully select which details to put on the page, using your narrator to frame them and provide continuity of story, without getting bogged down in minutiae.

EXERCISE 8: WORKING THIRD PERSON

You are probably writing a story right now, or you have ideas for one. If you have worked through *The Story Works Guide to Writing Character*, you have plenty of material in your journal. Grab your point of view character now, whichever one you want to work with. You're going to write him a scene.

1. Have your main character in mind. Now let's put him into conflict: he just got caught with his hand in the cookie jar. Make the figurative cookie jar, the character who caught him, and your protagonist's reason for digging in the cookie jar—wholly justified or a lapse of judgment—whatever you'd like.

2. Write a single, third person, past tense, limited point of view.

3. Make certain your narrator has a strong presence on the page. Describe. Expound. Reflect. Show.

4. I do not mean make your narrator a character the reader "sees" on the page. I mean do not write a scene that is entirely dialogue and characters moving around the stage of the page. Flex some narrative muscles. Include some details only the narrator can see. Think about the mood of the scene and how you want your readers to feel about the character and his world.

5. Open your journal and get your pencil ready. Set a timer for fifteen minutes. This is freewriting, so do not stop your hand moving. No matter what. Start the clock, and go!

6. Stop when the timer goes off. If you have a page of "I don't know what to write," try again. Otherwise, read it. Don't worry about whether or not it's good.

7. Answer the following questions in your journal:

   – Is the narrative voice distinct from the point of view character? How so?

   – What is the mood of the scene? How has the narrative voice established the mood?

   – Is the narrative distance close or distant? How does that affect the reader's relationship to the character? Do you want your reader to identify with or oppose your character's point of view? How did you accomplish that?

   – What has the narrator shown the reader and how might it affect the reader?

   – Overall, what are your impressions of this scene? What are the effects of the choices you made?

   – Was it easy or difficult to write? Why? How? What did you learn from this exercise?

RECAP

In this chapter, we examined the third person point of view.

- A close, limited, third person point of view is the most prevalent point of view today.

- With third person narratives, your narrator may be omniscient, like God, or a limited observer, like Margaret Mead.

- Because third person creates a separation between the narrative voice and the point of view character, the narrator can become invisible to the reader, like background music.

- In a single, third person point of view, point of view character and protagonist are synonyms. The point of view character must be changed by the events of the story.

- When writers try to track every move their character makes on the page, it creates a hyper-real writing style that slows the story's pace and can bore readers.

- Exercise 8: Working Third Person. In this exercise, you wrote and analyzed a third person scene, focusing on how your choices influenced your narrative presence.

Chapter 9

Keeping Them All Straight

MULTIPLE POINTS OF VIEW

When writers set out to write more than one point of view, they face certain challenges. The greatest challenge is, again, control. When we have the freedom to move through several or many characters' perspectives, we might be tempted to write fast and loose, following any character anywhere, however briefly, to show the reader this or that. The result is not compelling fiction, but sloppy writing. The number of point of view characters should be limited to those that are essential to the narrative. Limiting the cast list will create a tighter, faster-paced story with enhanced suspense and stronger *reveals,* in which the narrator provides answers to questions the reader has been prompted to ask.

MULTIPLE MISTAKES

With multiple point of view stories, there are often points of view that don't belong. A point of view must be earned, must be essential and justifiable, or it will create clutter and weak storytelling. When you write multiple points of view, you face several pitfalls as a writer. As we all know, pits are easy to fall into and hard to climb out of. Let's examine common errors with multiple points of view, so we can stay out of the pits altogether.

I am not against multiple point of view characters; I am against unearned point of view characters and sloppy writing.

Attachment Issues: When you have *too* many point of view characters in your story, some of them are not contributing to the story in a meaningful way. They are dead weight creating drag, instead of forward momentum. They need to be cut. One problem with too many point of view characters is that readers may have a tough time identifying the protagonist and attaching themselves to her. Without a clear and immediate main character, you risk readers not liking any one character enough to give your story her time and attention.

Your main character is the heart of the story, the vehicle that carries readers through the story. We need to find her likable and fascinating enough to stick with her. This is why, even with an ensemble cast of characters, there is typically one who serves as the focal point—the one the story and the other characters revolve around.

Develop control over a single point of view narrative, then expand your repertoire as appropriate to each story. When a story demands multiple point of view characters, keep only the *essential* ensemble members and let one character be the star.

Head Hopping: When transitions between point of view characters' perspectives lack clarity and purpose, you end up with *head hopping*, a phenomenon in which the point of view jumps, froglike, from one character to another without reason or control.

In head hopping, the characters seem to vie for position, each one scrapping over who "owns" what piece of the narrative. The reader hardly has a chance to be with one point of view character before being yanked out of that perspective and thrust into another. Chapters become dizzying rides on a merry-go-round as we skim across one perspective after another, without ever getting depth or meaning out of any of them.

Do not give your reader whiplash.

The solution to head hopping is the same as the solution to the attachment issue: less is more. By cutting the number of perspectives you can enter, you will force yourself to identify and control those that are necessary.

Say you have three perspectives you feel are vital. In order to write an easily tracked multiple, third person point of view, you will need to create clean shifts between perspectives. The best way to do this is to allow yourself only one point of view per chapter—or scene if required. Each shift in point of view will be marked by a chapter break or a line of white space, formatted to signal a scene break. You will also need to immediately identify the new point of view character at each shift.

Here are the first sentences of several chapters from *A Stone's Throw*. The point of view character is identified at the beginning of each chapter so the reader is always in the know.

Gemma lifted a bag of rice from the grocery shelf and considered its weight in her hands.

How do you know you're in love? Peter had believed himself in love with Gemma for years.

Simona pedaled through the city, bundled against the wind in a short coat and scarf

Not every chapter needs to name the point of view character in the first sentence, and it is good to vary things; however, as a rule you want to identify the point of view character as soon as possible, in the first few sentences. There is more room to play with your openings when the readers know the characters well enough to distinguish between them without names. For example, readers of *A Stone's Throw* know that Simona is a painter working on a commissioned mural in a women's resource center. Chapter eighteen begins this way:

The portrait was of a ragged woman with a dirt-encrusted face and torn clothes. The woman had white hair, bleached by hard years, and a permanent squint to her eyes. She was younger than she looked and older than she needed to be.

With a filthy cracked hand, she tugged on a lock of hair, pulled the thin section of scraggly strands so taut it stretched across the eye, along the nose, and past the purplish lips, threatening to break free from her scalp. The dismal eyes were vacant and the scarf that circled her neck full of holes. This one she called Medusa.

Simona sang the "Itsy Bitsy Spider" as she worked.

Here the character is not named until the second paragraph, but the second word, "portrait," identifies the point of view character as clearly as if I had opened with "Simona painted…"

Underdeveloped Characters: Let's look at the pyramid below. You may remember it from *The Story Works Guide to Writing Character.* We have the point of view character at the tip of the pyramid. Below that are the primary, or main supporting, characters. Below them are the secondary characters, who still get a name and dialogue, but are minor supporting characters. At the bottom of the pyramid is its broad base, the tertiary characters, the extras, those characters with descriptors like "lady with dog." The higher up the pyramid, the richer and deeper the character needs to be.

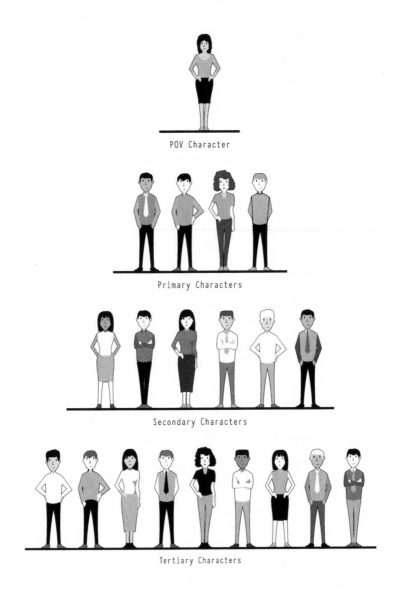

POV Character

Primary Characters

Secondary Characters

Tertiary Characters

If you lay the mantle "point of view" on one of your characters, you must now make that character come alive. The more point of view characters you put in your story, the harder you have to work to provide history, backstory, distinctive traits, motivation, goals, obstacles, and subplots. If you do not equally develop each point of view character, you will present your readers with disposable, ho-hum characters.

Honor your readers and your devotion to craft. Limit the number of points of view you have in your story to only those that are truly deserving of the intense development process that must go into any point of view character.

Quality over quantity.

Spoiler Alert: That extra, unearned perspective often does the story and reader a disservice, especially when the unearned perspective belongs to the antagonist.

As writers, we need to know what the bad guy is doing off the page when the good guy is on the page. The good guy can't know what the bad guy is doing. And the reader *shouldn't* know what the bad guy is doing. All too often, writers give the antagonist a point of view so that they can show the reader something going on behind the protagonist's back. This would be great generative writing, *for our eyes only.* A serious problem arises when writers use the antagonist's perspective in the story, because letting the reader in on our villain's nefarious deeds spoils the fun of reading the story. An example will make this clear.

Remember the film version of L. Frank Baum's *The Wizard of Oz?* Toto pulls back the curtain to reveal the man with the levers and buttons. Dorothy and her friends are shocked—and so is the audience—to discover that the Great and Powerful Oz is just smoke and mirrors. "Pay no attention to the man behind the curtain," Oz booms, while Dorothy watches the man speak those very words into a microphone on his console. Imagine if we, the audience, had been shown the man ducking behind the curtain and powering up his console before Dorothy and friends entered the chamber. We would know something she didn't, but we would know too much. We would know that she could take Oz in a fight, because he's not so great and powerful after all. As a result, we would not be on the same ride as Dorothy. We would not feel her intimidation and frustration, because we would know it is all a sham. Her discovery of the man behind the curtain would be old news to us, and we would be deprived of the fun of the surprising reveal. It does not matter how surprised your protagonist is if the reveal is old news to your reader.

> Writers can spoil their own reveals by giving away too much, and it happens most often through the antagonist's point of view.

The simplest way to avoid giving away too much is to not give your antagonist a perspective. There is no good reason to show readers what the antagonist is doing behind the scenes. Let the reader discover what has been going on when your protagonist does. That way, everyone will be surprised.

HOW TO SPOIL THE SPOILERS

Suppose your antagonist has earned his point of view? How do you give him a voice without creating spoilers? Carefully craft the antagonist's scenes to create *intrigue,* questions the reader must read on to have answered, and build tension.

As mentioned above, I gave the antagonist a point of view in my Skoghall Mystery Series. So how did I do it without creating spoilers? A better question is *why* did I do it?

In chapter seven, "The Right Point of View," I said your decisions could be based on craft, audience, and artistry. I did not give my antagonist a point of view so I could show the reader things the protagonist could not know. I did not give my antagonist a point of view so I could chronicle the story's action through every single step. I did it because I wanted to explore questions like, why would a person do these things? Just how terrifying *is* the human psyche? These are artistry reasons for giving my antagonist a perspective that in turn shaped how I crafted the story, which in turn shaped how my story affects readers.

Let's look at a mock example from *Dark Corners in Skoghall.* This is not what I wrote and published; it is something I wrote for purposes of illustrating this point. The antagonist, Ethan, is stalking the protagonist, Jess.

Ethan sat in a green pickup truck in front of the Skoghall Village Hall. In the passenger seat, Erick, whom he considered of limited intelligence and ambition, stared at his phone, overly interested in the moronic texts of his slut girlfriend. Ethan didn't enjoy keeping the company of fools, but he found it useful.

Ethan smacked the phone out of Erick's hands. It clattered against the dashboard before landing between Erick's feet. "Hey," Erick protested.

"Pay attention."

"To what? She went inside the café." Erick bent down, awkwardly twisting his long frame to reach between his knees and find his phone on the truck's gritty floor mat. "You're such a...," he muttered, letting his voice trail off.

Ethan decided to ignore it. There would be other opportunities to correct Erick, and Ethan enjoyed holding his temper in, so that when he unleashed it, it stunned whoever was on the receiving end. "I don't want to lose her."

Erick brushed off his phone, scowling, before sliding it into his pocket. "Yeah? Then what?"

"Then we follow her, dumbass. We find out where she lives, because that will give us the upper hand."

"Upper hand to do what?" Erick's voice rose with alarm. "Look. We did exactly what we set out to do, and look how well that turned out. *Not.* I don't want any more trouble, Ethan."

"We won't get into trouble. We'll just scare her a little. Maybe run her over just for the fun of it. But we won't have any—*more*—trouble."

This scene is all "on the nose." It is too *real,* too obvious, and gives away too much of what's to come. Knowing that Ethan is stalking Jess is enough to establish a creepy mood and get the readers worrying about what he's going to do next. The work of the scene, then, is not to belabor the point. It is to move beyond the point and reveal something new that enhances the reader's understanding of the character or the situation.

Let's look at what I actually wrote for this scene.

Ethan sat in a green pickup truck in front of the Skoghall Village Hall. In the passenger seat, Erick, whom he considered of limited intelligence and ambition, stared at his phone, overly interested in the moronic texts of his slut girlfriend. Ethan didn't enjoy keeping the company of fools, but he found it useful. Being...well, being *him,* required a certain degree of solitariness. He knew he was still young, which was partly why he was being so ambitious now, but he'd lived long enough to know that most people didn't think the way he did. Most people would be appalled by his actions, but that was only because they were limited in the scope of their...scope.

Sometimes he felt like he was drifting on high, above it all, but also beyond it all. He saw the pointlessness of everything. He also saw the incredible sad beauty of it. He remembered a particularly windy day when he was a child—one of those days when trees shake and wind chimes are clanged about in a way that is anything but melodic and beneath all the other sounds is the sound of leaves dry as paper skittering down the pavement. He sat on his front stoop breaking a fresh stick of sidewalk chalk into little nubs, and he saw a plastic bag blow by. A short while later, a piece of newspaper. And after that, a crunched-up beer can skidded past. He realized then that if there was a God in Heaven who had created this place called Eden, He had since abandoned it to His low-rent tenants. And those tenants, they were trashing the place.

And if there was no God in Heaven to look down upon him, to witness his every thought (which was what his mother told him every single night), then there was only himself to know what he was up to, only himself to hold him accountable. The thrill of it surged through his body with such sudden force that his bladder emptied, right there on the concrete steps of his stoop. Since nobody was there to witness it, not even God, it did not count against him. Instead of flushing with shame, the way he'd been taught, he flushed with a secret pride and his first inkling of power. He remained on those steps, crumbling his red stick of chalk into powder, sitting in his wet shorts. He wanted to see if someone would come and notice, if there would be any punishment. Finally, he stood up, wiped the chalk dust from his hands onto the front of his shorts, and went inside for a snack.

His mother noticed the chalk, for which he was lightly scolded. She did not notice the urine that had dried in his shorts. If she had, she would have paddled him.

That was the start of his great experiment. And this... how to characterize this? He stared across the street, through the haze of heat that glazed the pavement, at the community garden, watching the woman talk to a man with a dog. This marked the end of his apprenticeship. In six weeks he'd turn eighteen and, with this project successfully completed, he'd declare himself a master.

Which scene is more revealing? More effective? Both are in Ethan's perspective. In both, the action is the same: he's sitting in his truck with his accomplice, stalking Jess. In the first, he essentially tells the reader what she already knows, that he is following Jess because he's planning to hurt her, which is implied by his stalking her. By telling the reader what's coming, the tension drops off to everyone's detriment. Jess might not know what's coming, but it's not her tension I'm trying to raise; it's the reader's. In the published excerpt, we follow Ethan into his memories while he watches Jess across the road. By leaving the action, which is only a guy sitting in a truck with another guy, to go into his thoughts, we delve deeper into Ethan's psyche. Going into his memories fulfills my artistic purpose of exploring what kind of person could become a killer. It also enhances the creepiness of the scene and raises the tension.

What makes you more worried for Jess? Knowing that a young man in a truck is following her? Or knowing that *that* young man is following her, the one who basically dared God to punish him as a boy?

To test the necessity of a point of view character's perspective to your story, ask yourself the following:

- Is this scene, in this character's perspective, telling the reader something she already knows or can easily infer?
- Is the scene broadcasting something about to happen, creating a spoiler?
- Is the scene emotionally flat, doing nothing much to enhance the reader's experience of the action or character?
- Would the story be tighter, better paced, and have more dramatic tension without this scene?

If you answered any of these questions with a yes, you need to revise or cut the scene. Or cut the character's perspective.

DRAMATIC TENSION AND REVEALS

In my example above, the reader knows that Jess will be all right. She might get hurt, but I'm not going to kill my protagonist in book two of a new series. If I do my job right as the author, the reader will worry about Jess nonetheless. Dramatic tension is created when you know that *something* is coming, but do not know what. If you don't know what is looming, you can't prepare for it, and that creates tension in anyone, including your readers.

For example, remember taking a big test? Maybe a college entrance exam? You knew, if you thought about it, that the test was not going to make or break your life. You would not cease to exist no matter the results. Yet the weeks of waiting between taking the test and receiving the score were agonizing, weren't they? Every time the test crossed your mind or someone mentioned college, your stomach twisted a little.

As writers, we manipulate stakes and tension in order to create low-level anxiety in the reader. For the reader, being absorbed by the tension is fun—unlike in real life. *Stakes* are what the character stands to gain or lose as a result of the situation. *Tension* is what the reader feels as a result of caring about that character's stakes.

> The reason a reader stays up
> half the night to finish a book
> is because the tension compelled
> her to keep turning pages.

In the first version of the scene above, Ethan tells the reader that he's going to try to run Jess over. That broadcasts the trouble Jess will soon face, which reduces the anxiety the reader feels. Knowing what's coming for your protagonist spoils the low-level anxiety associated with the need to find out what is going to happen next.

A reveal can be small or large. In the second version of the scene above, I set up that Ethan is stalking Jess and he's going to harm her. The reader is now anticipating the fulfillment of that setup, which creates intrigue. The reveal occurs when Ethan runs Jess and her dog off the road. The reveal satisfies the dramatic tension and concludes that movement within the story. Reveals are a storyteller's currency. Spend them wisely.

> A reveal is to dramatic tension
> what a punch line is to a joke.

MULTIPLE ARCS

When we discuss character arcs, we often talk about the point of view character as the one, singular, deserving of a character arc. In a multiple point of view story, however, not every point of view character needs to be changed forever by the events of the story. It depends on the story and your reasons for giving those characters a point of view.

In *A Stone's Throw,* all three of my point of view characters are forever changed and all three have character arcs. Peter's point of view is not equal to Simona's and Gemma's, so his perspective and his arc do not receive equal attention, but he *does* have one. In the Skoghall Mystery Series, the antagonists and victims receive points of view, but not arcs. My purpose in giving them perspectives is to explore certain questions, not to follow their growth as human beings.

When you write multiple point of view characters, your protagonist must have an arc. If you have multiple protagonists, they must have arcs. As for the others, it depends. What is their role in the story? How much of the story is devoted to their perspectives? How much will readers care about them? A simple way to think about this is by placing your characters on the character pyramid. If they are primary supporting characters, like Peter, they deserve full development and an arc. If they are secondary supporting characters, like my antagonists and victims, they do not require an arc.

Protagonist(s)

Primary Characters

Secondary Characters

Tertiary Characters

Once you've decided who's primary and who's secondary, do a head count. If the top tiers (protagonist and primary) of the pyramid are looking crowded, consider demoting a few characters.

WHEN YOU JUST GOTTA HAVE 'EM

Now you know that less is more, head hopping is bad, and an unearned point of view character's perspective can ruin your dramatic tension. But you've got a story that absolutely must have an ensemble cast of point of view characters. How do you work with so many point of view characters without climbing out of one pit only to fall into another?

Let's say you have an ensemble cast of heroes and villains from multiple camps, like the Werewolves and the Zombies. You need to show things happening in each camp at various times, so you are going to need one point of view character from each camp.

What if you decide to give all of your primary characters a point of view? How will you keep them all straight? How will the reader know which character to focus on or root for? You need to create a hierarchy of point of view characters and, for each scene, consider their necessity.

For example, suppose the Werewolves and Zombies are going into battle and my hierarchy of characters looks like this:

- Werewolves: Walter (1) > Wendy (2) > Winston (3) > Whimsy (4) > Wendell (5)
- Zombies: Zelda (1) > Zinnia (2) > Zephyr (3) > Zeus (4) > Zena (5)

When all of these characters are going to be in a battle scene, things are likely to get messy, for you and the reader. If a scene is messy for the reader, you can bet the reader is confused. A confused reader is a dissatisfied reader.

Which point of view should you use? According to the hierarchy, Walter (1) and Zelda (1) trump everyone else.

But you don't want to head hop, so do you choose Walter or Zelda? That depends. Here is where necessity comes into the equation. Ask yourself the following:

- What is the purpose of this scene? The reader's takeaway?
- For which character are the stakes higher right now?
- Who will the reader be rooting for?

In an epic battle, the battle might need to be shown in multiple parts, with several point of view characters contributing different perspectives to the battle's drama.

Suppose Winston (3) is fighting Zena (5). Winston trumps Zena, so use his point of view.

Meanwhile, Whimsy (4) and Wendell (5) are sneaking around the edges of the battle with some dynamite. Although neither of these characters is high in the hierarchy, they are the only ones sneaking around the main battle. If it is necessary to show the dynamite in play, you'll need one of these points of view. Whimsy trumps Wendell, so use her point of view.

Zinnia (2) fights Winston (3) to the death and wins. Here Zinnia trumps Winston, but a death scene is naturally high drama, and life or death is as high as stakes get, so you might be justified in showing that segment of the battle from Winston's point of view. If the reader is going to be rooting for, and therefore lament the loss of Winston, his point of view will definitely have more dramatic appeal. If the reader is going to be rooting for Zinnia, you might want to use her point of view and make the fight close.

By considering your ensemble point of view characters this way, you will be less likely to head hop and more likely to choose the right perspective for the scene. The right choice accounts for the character's role in the story, necessity, and the most dramatic and tension-inducing perspective on the action.

You can read an excerpt of a werewolf-zombie battle from Chris Fox's *No Mere Zombie* in the special section, "Name That Point of View," toward the back of this book.

EXERCISE 9: CHOOSING THE BEST POINT OF VIEW CHARACTER

If you have a story with multiple point of view characters, you can use it for this exercise. If you don't, I encourage you to do the exercise anyway. It will help you understand what makes a point of view character the *right* point of view character for a given scene. If you are not using your own work in progress, think of your favorite television show with an ensemble cast of characters. It will give you familiar material to work with for this exercise.

1. Write down your protagonist's name at the top of your list. Beneath it, make a list of all other point of view characters.

2. Jot down a few words or sentences for each of the characters that define their roles in the story.

3. Assign each of the characters a station in the hierarchy. Base it on their importance to the story, how likable they are, and their longevity in the story or series. This may seem a bit arbitrary now. That's all right. Work with it.

4. Invent a scenario that will involve all of the characters that can play out over several scenes. Here are a few ideas that require a coordinated group effort and can use different mini-settings within a larger setting:

   - They need to don disguises and infiltrate the villain's lair.
   - They need to create distractions and steal top secret documents during a political event.
   - They need to swarm a bank and free hostages while taking down the bad guys.

5. Outline the scenario so you know how many scenes need to occur, how many settings you'll require, and which characters need to be involved in each scene. Possible scenes:

   - Distract security guards.
   - Crack a safe.
   - Sneak past the security cameras.
   - Defuse the bomb.
   - Rescue the captives.
   - Guide hostages to safety.
   - Fight the villains.
   - Hack the computer.

6. With your outline and cast of characters, it is time to divide and conquer. Split up your characters so the scenes can be acted out by the various players. Spend some time thinking about which characters to place in which scene. If you've

got one character who can pick locks and crack safes, put him in the safe cracking scene. If you've got one who's a black belt in karate, she should be in position to take out the thugs guarding the captives.

7. Any time your protagonist is on the page, he gets the point of view. In those other scenes, however, where it could go two or three ways, see if the hierarchy provides an easy answer. Joe, who's been on the team since book one, trumps Sally, who joined the team in book three.

8. When the answer isn't as simple as who has top rank, start asking questions about the tension you want the scene to elicit from your reader and which character can best deliver.

    –   Say Joe and Sally are cornered and in a skirmish with the villains. Joe is going to die and Sally is going to escape.

    –   If you want the reader to experience the moment of Joe's death in the most profoundly moving way, then put us in his perspective.

    –   If you want the reader to experience Sally's mistake and resultant survivor's guilt, use her perspective.

    –   If you want us to be uncertain whether or not Sally screwed up, use Joe's perspective, and show us Sally's role through his eyes with enough ambiguity to raise questions.

    –   If you want Joe to pass the torch to Sally, so that she can go forward as his replacement on the team and in the readers' hearts, use her perspective to establish her courage and loyalty.

- If you want Joe to save Sally and die a hero, you could use either perspective effectively.

9. Set a timer for fifteen minutes and freewrite your scene in one point of view character's perspective.

10. Reset the timer for fifteen minutes. This time use the other point of view character's perspective.

11. Compare the scenes. Answer these questions in your journal:

- What are the different traits each character brings to the scene? One might be technical, the other emotive. One experienced, the other a rookie. One cocky, the other nervous.

- Which point of view character best advances the story in the direction you need it to go?

- How can you use your point of view character to set up intrigue? Create tension? Establish certain facts? Or obscure certain facts?

- How does the scene change with the point of view character?

Frequently, a scene could be presented effectively from multiple characters' perspectives. The one you choose, however, will determine the shape of the scene and its impact on the reader.

Get your Choose the Right Point of View Character worksheet at www. WordEssential.com/JoinStoryWorksPOV.

Note: Barbara Kingsolver's *The Poisonwood Bible* is a powerful example of a multiple point of view novel. Four sisters each have perspectives throughout, and their mother has a few chapters as well. The point of view characters are delineated by chapters. The setting is confined and the characters are a family, living together through the same set of circumstances. Yet each character contributes a unique outlook, enhancing the reader's experience of this story. As you read it, ask yourself, why this character for this scene? You will further develop your understanding of the power of perspective upon a story.

RECAP

In this chapter, we explored how to work with multiple point of view characters and how to avoid the common pitfalls of having multiple perspectives in a story.

- Limiting the number of point of view characters in a story creates a tighter, faster-paced story with enhanced suspense and stronger reveals.
- When there is no clear protagonist in a story, readers won't know which character is the heart of the story, leading to a lack of attachment to the protagonist.
- With too many point of view characters, the writer risks head hopping, jumping from one perspective to another, without giving the reader the chance to experience any of them.

- When you write multiple point of view characters, establish clear rules for how you transition between them. The simplest rule to follow is one point of view character per chapter.
- You must always signal whose perspective the reader is entering when a shift occurs, typically within the first sentence or two.
- Developing a point of view character is a lot of work. If some of that development gets neglected, the characters seem like shadows of each other.
- Using unearned point of view characters to show the reader things happening behind the protagonist's back can spoil your reveals and reduce the reader's enjoyment of the story.
- If you are writing an ensemble cast, create a hierarchy to help you choose quickly and easily which point of view character to use for each scene.
- Exercise 9: Choosing the Best Point of View. In this exercise, you played with an ensemble cast and practiced deciding who gets a scene and why.
- When you are in doubt about which point of view character to use, assess what each character can bring to the scene and the dramatic effect that perspective can create.

Chapter 10

Playing God

THE OMNISCIENT POINT OF VIEW

An omniscient narrator, or narrative voice, is like God: all-knowing and all-seeing, can enter the consciousness of any story element she chooses, from a person to a rock, and is not bound by time and space.

An omniscient narrator can enter many characters' heads. But she may choose to enter only a select few. In doing so, she will exercise her omniscience, making connections the characters could not make, knowing things they could not know, and remarking on things outside the bounds of the story's time and space. It is in exercising these powers that the omniscient narrator differs from the multiple, third person, limited narrator.

LIMITED-WHAT?

We find the term limited-omniscient in literary theory, and I am mentioning it here to acknowledge its existence. For our purposes, I am going to dismiss the term limited-omniscient. I find it to be an oxymoron. You either are or are not omniscient. Being a mind reader does not make one God. And your narrator will be *either* omniscient *or* limited.

When someone mentions the limited-omniscient, they probably mean a narrator with a limited scope of knowledge using the traditional authorial voice to tell the story to the reader. In other words, a distant, third person point of view. Again, I mention it here to be thorough in my discussion of point of view, but now I invite you to put the term limited-omniscient out of your mind.

KEEP YOUR OPINIONS TO YOURSELF...OR NOT

Your omniscient narrator will be either an *authorial* narrator or an *essayist* narrator.

The authorial-omniscient narrator is the classic literary storyteller. He is invisible, respectable, and formal. He narrates from on high. The authorial-omniscient narrator might sound old-fashioned, but he doesn't have to be. The authorial-omniscient voice is one we are all comfortable with as a literary device. In fact, any time you write an invisible narrator, you are exercising your authorial voice, whether omniscient or limited.

The essayist-omniscient narrator is a personal storyteller. This narrator has a stronger presence on the page, because we sense his personality. He might be academic or casual. He exercises his opinions and freely passes judgment. He is still all-knowing and all-seeing. He still enters any perspective he chooses to, from person to rock, but he gets personal.

Let's look at an example. I will work with the tale "Hansel and Gretel."

Authorial-Omniscient

Once upon a time, there lived a poor woodsman in a great forest. His wife died and left him with the care of two young children. A boy, named Hansel, and a pretty little girl, named Gretel. The woodsman could hardly leave young children to fend for themselves each day while he went to work, his axe propped upon his shoulder, and so he was in a hurry to marry again and provide them with a mother.

This he did, quickly enough. And he felt a great relief the day he brought his beautiful, young bride to his cottage deep in the forest. The woodsman was all smiles as he introduced her to his children, saying, "Children, this is your new mother." But the children saw something in her that frightened them. Though they could not explain it, it is well known that children are able to sense the sort of heart a person has within, and the new mother's heart was no bigger than a walnut and just as hard. Gretel took her brother's hand and refused to speak.

By the time the full moon shone again upon their little clearing, the woodsman had fallen deeply in love with his wife. He adored her immensely and fawned over her so much that she had to send him off to the forest each day with smiles and fond promises. But the moment the door shut on the little cottage, her figure changed. She became sour and bitter. She loosened the laces on her bodice and let her hair fall in tangles over her shoulders. She ordered the children to do her chores, chores fit for a grown woman that no true mother would force upon her children.

Essayist-Omniscient

Ah, but she was no true mother. Her heart had once been broken, turning her into a selfish and cruel woman who used her wiles to bend her husband to her every whim. She knew no other way to behave and had been behaving this way so long that she was past redemption. There was only one thing that would put an end to her miserable cruelty. Unfortunately for Hansel and little Gretel, the woman had enough time remaining to turn her spite against them.

A porcelain figurine of a beautiful shepherdess stood on the mantel over the fireplace. It had belonged to the children's mother. Gretel imagined her mother watching over them from the eyes of the shepherdess. The little figurine, though not their mother, did watch over them. So miserable was she at the children's plight that she longed for the power to shed tears.

The horrible woman stopped feeding the children whenever their father was off in the woods. And when he was home, she only gave them the smallest of portions. The woodsman, besotted with his bride and blind to her cruelty, did not take notice until the children were stick-thin and their eyes bulged over sallow cheeks. "My love," he said, "why have the children grown so thin?"

She answered that he was not providing enough for them to eat. She worked her charms on him until she had him convinced that the only way any of them would survive the winter was if he led the children into the forest and abandoned them. Her heart was no bigger than a walnut and just as hard, for she thought only of herself and could not imagine the joy of a family.

In both examples, the narrator moves fluidly between the characters' perspectives and reports things only an omniscient narrator could know. In the first example, the narrator remarks upon the special ability of children to know the shape of a person's heart—an observation outside the scope of the specific story. In the second example, the narrator tells us the stepmother's heart had once been broken, which is a jump in time to report something outside the frame of the story. He also enters the perspective of the figurine on the mantel.

The authorial-omniscient narrator presents the story to the reader without personality or judgment. The authorial-omniscient narrator reports on the stepmother's heart, but does so simply as another fact for the reader to judge for herself. The essayist-omniscient narrator makes use of judgmental adjectives, like "horrible woman." He also has a rather informal voice, "ah, but," and "she worked her charms on him." We feel he is speaking directly to the reader, instead of speaking from on high. Because we are already attuned to the essayist-omniscient narrator's voice, when he says her heart was no bigger than a walnut and just as hard, it feels like a condemnation. This voice and these judgments inform the reader how she should feel about the characters and events, something the impartial authorial-omniscient narrator does not do.

Some Essayists Are Bigger than Others

The essayist-omniscient narrator has personality and values he is free to share with the reader. He may have a minor presence on the page, as above. Or he might have a large personality. The essayist-omniscient narrator is a persona of the author. He is not a character, because he does not appear and act in the story with the real characters. Let's see how a big persona might retell "Hansel and Gretel."

Come and gather 'round. I have a tale for you of a father blinded first by grief and then by trickery, of the cruelty of a woman without a heart, and of dear, clever little children.

Not all women are fit to be mothers, as you well know, and this one in particular was a real witch. I would like to call her a witch, but actually it does a disservice to witches. For this woman was a class unto herself. So beautiful and so cruel was she, and all without the aid of magic.

The essayist-omniscient narrator is a persona of the author, not a character.

WHY WOULD YOU?

Since the omniscient point of view is so seldom used in contemporary fiction, why would you want to use it? An omniscient point of view can be effective in certain genres of story, like the tale and the epic. It can also be effective when the setting functions as a character. Or when the story spans generations. Or when the scope of the story is greater than the characters could ever realize. As mentioned before, Edward P. Jones's *The Known World* is a wonderful example of the omniscient narrator.

HOW COULD YOU?

Omniscient is not the right point of view for most stories, but when it is, it can be wonderful. You might feel the omniscient point of view is right for your story because of the kind of story you want to tell, your artistic goals, or an omniscient narrator might simply be how you "hear" the story.

I had been planning to write an omniscient story for artistic reasons, when a trip to the beach presented me with material for a story that could only be told in the omniscient point of view. "The Herd" is about a lot of people on a beach, rather like a herd of antelope on a savannah. And there is a predator on the beach, rather like a lion on said savannah. I wanted to write a story featuring herd mentality, so the authorial-omniscient narrator was the obvious choice.

More than any other point of view, omniscient requires careful control, because you do not have the clear parameters of this or that character's head. You can slip in and out of any character's perspective at will, jump forward and backwards in time, and even show the perspective of the chair in the corner, if you so choose.

As you know, the cardinal rule of story craft is: you can write whatever you want, so long as you do it well. Doing it well means making your rules, establishing them up front for the reader, and then consistently abiding by them.

As "The Herd" grew into a collection of stories, I knew I would write each of them in the authorial-omniscient, present tense point of view. But no other story would be set on the beach with all of those characters. To maintain and control my point of view as I expanded the collection, I established these rules:

- The narrator can and will, at least once in each story, reference something outside the scope of the story itself, thus establishing that she is not bound by time and space.
- The narrator will inhabit the perspectives of at least two point of view characters in each story—while she can enter any and every head on the page, she will only enter those that effectively advance the story.
- The narrator will be dispassionate and reliable, while entering the perspectives of characters who are subjective and not necessarily reliable.

- When shifting between characters' perspectives, my narrator will do so fluidly when characters share a relationship and common space. I will format the story so that the shift is visually represented by a line of white space between paragraphs when the characters do not share common space. For example, when shifting between the perspectives of a couple sharing a beach towel, the shift is fluid. When moving from them to another character who is a stranger to them—sharing the beach, but not personal space—I use the visual cue of a line of white space.

These rules established a narrative framework for my stories that immediately established the omniscient point of view for the reader.

Let's look at an excerpt from "The Herd" to see how the shifts in perspective are handled.

Rey and Tegan stand up on their towels, tucking their magazines under their beach bags so they won't blow away, then Tegan starts toward the water. She has a walk she has been working on. She drags the tips of her toes through the sand as she steps forward, making certain to cross one foot in front of the other. Also, one hand rests lightly, jauntily, upon her hip. She has taken some dance classes and watches models on the catwalk on YouTube. These are the sources of her new affectation. Rey has held back so that she can look down at her cousin. "Well?" she says. "Are you coming in with us?" Her hips are cocked, but this is not an affectation. This is a display of her impatience with and disapproval of Suzie.

Suzie shrugs. "Okay."

A man on the beach watches the girls enter the water. He watches Suzie especially. He likes her plumpness. This man does not understand why she is self-conscious, but he understands vulnerability. He watches Suzie enter the water. Her friends run in, squealing and splashing, but she steps in, hesitantly, testing her way.

A little boy wearing water wings scoops sand into a pail at the edge of the water. Suzie comes dangerously close to stepping in the hole he is digging, to collapsing its sidewall. He looks up, but cannot see Suzie's face because of the sun. It forces him to close his eyes completely and drop his head. Thomas is a serious boy, which is why his parents call him Thomas, not Tom and certainly not Tommy. His entire world is that hole in the sand. He hopes that if he digs deep enough he will find a crab, or perhaps a mermaid. He reminds himself that mermaids live in deep waters with the bass and walleye that his grandpa pulls out of the lake. He is, therefore, unlikely to find a mermaid in his hole. *But*, he thinks, *I might find a mermaid's skull!* and he continues to dig. He will dig with perfect concentration until he gets bored, or until his mother calls him back to the blanket for a snack.

Published in *Water~Stone Review*, vol.16.

CHAPTER 10: PLAYING GOD

Controlling your narrative means every choice you make is guided by its relevance and how it advances the story. Is that chair's perspective important to the story? Does it advance us toward a climactic moment of some kind? If so, then ask, when is the chair's perspective most relevant? Is it an amusing voice appropriate to hear throughout? Should the chair come in after the old woman who sat in it dies?

Because an omniscient point of view means working with multiple point of view characters, you can apply the same questions that guide multiple points of view to the omniscient point of view. Ask yourself, in this scene, which point of view is highest ranking? Which perspective is most relevant? Which best advances the story? And, if I use this perspective, how will it enhance my dramatic and thematic goals? By answering those questions, you will develop your understanding of when to use which point of view.

And don't forget to assess whether each point of view character should have an arc or not. Any protagonist must have a character arc. Primary supporting characters deserve them as well. It is possible to have secondary supporting characters, especially in the omniscient, who have a perspective, but not an arc.

WHAT MAKES THE OMNISCIENT HARD?

Writing in the omniscient can feel like writing without boundaries, which can lead to random, sloppy ventures into various perspectives. With freedom comes responsibility. Your responsibility is to weave a tight narrative so the reader does not become confused. Confusion is your archenemy. If a reader pauses in your narrative to wonder what you meant or how that's possible or where that character came from, you risk losing him. He might not know why he's abandoning the story; it simply won't feel right. The story might meander without a clear direction. Or there might not be a character to whom he can relate.

If you're considering an omniscient narrator for your story, consider whether this is the *best* possible way to tell the story. Account for genre, the main character's arc (or characters' arcs), the plot arc, and if the special features of the omniscient point of view are necessary for your story.

EXERCISE 10: THE GREAT AND POWERFUL YOU

Ready to exercise your omniscient muscles? You may want to take a look at the "Hansel and Gretel" passages and the excerpt from "The Herd" again. Note the way the omniscient is used in each passage, the difference between authorial- and essayist-omniscient narrators, and how the narrative moves between characters' heads.

1. Choose a fairy tale. Any one will do. They lend themselves well to the omniscient, being tales. Don't look it up. It doesn't matter if you're true to the story or go off in a new direction. Have fun with it.

2. Write an adaptation of the tale using an omniscient narrator. Set your timer for fifteen minutes. Ready? Go!

3. Read what you wrote. Answer these questions in your journal:

- Did you write an authorial- or essayist-omniscient narrator?
- Why? Was it something you thought about before you began, or did you slip into that voice naturally?
- Which of the powers did you use in this brief passage of freewriting? Time jumps? Setting or object perspectives? Generalizations and reflections outside the scope of the story?
- Make some notes about the process of writing in the omniscient. Was it fun? Hard? What did you learn?

4. Set your timer and get your pen. If you wrote in the authorial-omniscient, write in the essayist-omniscient this time. If there are any powers you did not use in the last session, make sure you use them this time. Go!

5. Read what you wrote.
   - Reflect on how this passage differs from the first. Compare the voice and its impact on you as a reader.
   - Was this narrator fun to write? Hard? What did you learn?

RECAP

In this chapter, we examined the omniscient point of view and how it differs from a multiple, third person point of view. The omniscient narrator has special powers that distinguish her from a limited narrator.

- The omniscient narrator is all-knowing and all-seeing, able to enter the perspective of any story element, from a person to a rock, and is outside the bounds of time and space.
- A narrator is either omniscient or limited.
- Your omniscient narrator can be authorial-omniscient, a neutral voice from on high, or essayist-omniscient, an opinionated storyteller.
- Omniscient works well for certain types of stories, like tales and epics. It is also useful when the setting functions as a character or the story spans generations.
- The omniscient narrator has special powers the limited narrator does not. Those powers distinguish him from other narrators. Thus, if you are to write in the omniscient, you must exercise some powers of omniscience.
- Omniscient point of view stories require even more control than limited point of view stories, because the narrator has full freedom of movement within the story.
- Shifts between characters' perspectives should be immediately, clearly indicated to the reader, whether those shifts occur fluidly within a paragraph or are separated with visual cues.
- Exercise 10: The Great and Powerful You. In this exercise, you wrote two scenes, one with an authorial-omniscient narrator and one with an essayist-omniscient narrator, flexing those extraordinary narrative muscles.

Chapter 11

It's Mine, All Mine

MIRROR, MIRROR ON THE WALL, IS FIRST PERSON THE CLOSEST POINT OF VIEW OF ALL?

New writers often gravitate toward first person, because if you are inside the character's head, it feels natural to show what the character is thinking, feeling, and experiencing. A first person narrative can lull you into complacency, believing you have done your authorial job because you have written something diary-like. Furthermore, it may seem that if you write in the first person, you do not need to have a separate narrative voice. Or perhaps you are not thinking about the narrator at all, because she's rolled up in the character, and as a result, you lose the distinction between character and narrator. That can create a flat, uninteresting story. Writing first person narratives carries as much responsibility and nuance as other points of view.

Have you ever watched the extras on a DVD of an animated movie and seen footage of the voice actors in a recording studio? It's fun to watch the actors with their headphones and microphones for the few minutes included on the DVD, but you would not want to watch the entire story that way. When a first person point of view does not distinguish between narrator and character, it's like watching voice actors. We get dialogue and conflict, even some action, but we miss out on the world that surrounds the characters.

When the narrator fails at his job, the reader is left with hundreds of pages of anecdotal storytelling, instead of a fully realized narrative journey complete with setting, action, mood, and voice. Many characters are not good storytellers (as you'll see in the discussion throughout this chapter), and it is your job as the writer to make that determination in the prewriting stages of your novel's development.

That is the downside of a first person narrative, the prerequisite cautionary statement. Now, let's discuss the upside.

ME, MYSELF, AND I

The first person narrative point of view is a good choice for a story when the protagonist is uniquely qualified to tell her own story. That is, she must be a competent and engaging storyteller.

A competent first person narrator distinguishes between the storyteller and the story-actor, providing a fully realized scene on every page.

When you have a character who can handle the job of narrator, you can create a narrative that

- feels more intimate than the third person, because the relationship between the reader and narrator is implied with the use of first person pronouns;
- heightens the personal, because the narrator has lived, not witnessed, the events of the story;
- creates a perspective based on hindsight that no other narrator could supply, because the first person narrator has survived, processed, and grown from the events of the story; or
- in the case of a present tense narrative, heightens the sense of immediacy, because the narrator is telling the story as it happens.

These are compelling reasons to use a first person point of view. Who wouldn't want a story to feel more intimate, personal, and have great hindsight or immediate perspective?

Before you decide first person wins the blue ribbon, keep in mind that I said it *feels* more intimate. It is not a fact; it is a sensation. Each point of view has compelling reasons to choose it. Listen to your story, the one in your gut and your heart. Test your inclinations. Then get writing in the best point of view for this particular story. Now, let's see if first person will work for you.

THE QUALIFIED CHARACTER

Why would a character have to tell the story herself? That may be one of those things you just know as the author. When I had my thesis meeting for my MFA program, one of my advisors asked me why I'd chosen a first person point of view for my historical novel *Saving Annabelle.* I told her it was how I heard the story. That being said, you still have to assess your character's narrative prowess. If she doesn't stand up to your careful scrutiny, take the role of narrator off her hands. I'll explain my choice in just a moment, so you can see whether "how I heard the story" stands up to scrutiny.

> The first person point of view
> is best used when the character
> must tell the story herself.

Not every character knows how to tell a story, because in order to tell a story in first person, the character has to be both the actor in the now of the story *and* the narrator in the later of the story.

In *Saving Annabelle,* Greta is telling the story from a hilltop while she watches her family's house burn down, which is the climax of the book, so her emotional distance from the events of the story is small. The story, however, spans twelve years, so her chronological distance from the events of the story varies.

Let's assess my choice to let Greta tell her own story. Qualities that make Greta a good choice for first person narrator:

- She has a beautiful use of language.
- She is an astute observer with a good memory.
- She reports things accurately.
- She is able to *show*.
- She can separate herself as narrator from herself as actor; Greta on the hilltop telling the story can narrate an emotional scene from her past with both feeling and perspective.
- And perhaps most compelling to me as the author, Greta owns this story. She would not have *allowed* anyone else to tell it. Greta exists in relation to the people and events such that she is uniquely able to tell the story.

When you consider telling a story in the first person, you need to assess your narrator the way I have Greta. If he lacks the necessary traits and skills to function as an effective narrator, you would be better off writing in the third person point of view. An example might help you see these narrative qualities on the page.

This excerpt from *Saving Annabelle* focuses on action and dialogue, not setting, so you can see that narrative prowess is about more than describing the scenery once or twice in a chapter. As you read it, note that Greta, the actor, is only ten years old, but the narrative voice remains consistently that of the mature Greta. Even in a scene busy with characters moving about the page and talking to each other, the narrator takes the time to notice and describe the characters, action, and setting. The reader is thus able to picture the tobacco juice in the driver's mustache, the mail pouches on the floor of the coach, and, although the ladies were described previously in the scene, the reader senses the social divide between the driver and the women through their speech and manners.

I ran out of the store and did not stop until I stood beside Lucy, who supervised our luggage being loaded into the boot.

"Thank you, Charlie," Lucy said, and handed him money for our tickets.

He stuffed the bills into the guard's bag hanging at his hip, then extracted a watch from his pants pocket and squinted at its face. I imagined that his eyes had filled with dust over the long trip down from St. Paul. Our driver wore bushy red sideburns that covered his jaw. His square face, ruddy in complexion, maintained the serious look of a man out to beat time.

"Ma'am," he muttered and then put his hand to the brim of his hat, though he did not actually tip it. "We'll be leavin' bout ten minutes. Soon as my teamster lad an' your smithy get the horses swapped out." I noticed when he turned his head to look toward the livery that his lower lip was swollen with a plug of tobacco.

"Sir, our mail," I said, presenting the pouch to him.

He looked at me as the brown tobacco juices bubbled from the corner of his mouth to collect in the whiskers of his mustache. He then looked in a small journal pulled from his vest pocket. "Nothin' for Landmark today."

Lucy stepped back from the coach, and I tugged on her sleeve. "Lucy," I whispered, "do you know him well?"

"Certainly not."

"But you called him Charlie. You know his Christian name."

She smiled at me. "Silly child. Charlie is another way of saying driver. I think it sounds much nicer to call him by Charlie than Driver, as though he had not a name at all."

I had seen the express coach come through town on occasion, but had never inspected it up close. Tin boxes large enough they required two men to handle were strapped to the roof. Inside the coach, we found much of the floor stacked with mail pouches. We were fortunate there were not any passengers already aboard, or we would not have fit inside. The coach rocked front to back as Charlie climbed onto his seat.

The expressman hollered loudly while we were still trying to settle in amidst the baggage. "Dash it, boy! Get on up you no-account mudsill."

Mother gasped and clamped her hands over my ears, but it was no use and I started a fit of giggling as the teamster, a raggedly filthy boy of no more than fourteen, set the coach rocking.

"Don't be so huffy at me," he exclaimed, as he climbed shotgun to Charlie.

Only Lucy seemed unaffected. "Oh, Maude," she sighed, "I have had necessity to ride many a coach, and that is the least of what I have heard. I stopped blushing long ago, and now I simply feign deafness."

THE IMPORTANCE OF VOICE

Your character's voice might be academic, literary, youthful, down-homey, unrefined, or any other characteristic that is appropriate to the character and the story. If you have a first person narrator, his narrative voice should sound like it belongs to that character. If your narrative sounds like it slipped out of someone else's mouth, you do not have an appropriate and believable voice for your narrator.

While they are the same person, they are not. Your character and first person narrator are two different entities. Chronological distance will shape the narrative, creating the distinction between actor and narrator. While that time was passing, of course your narrator was busy living. When you choose the chronological distance between your narrator and character, you must decide how much has happened in your narrator's life to temper his perspective on the events of the *now*-story. In the excerpt above, my narrator's voice should sound like a mature, refined version of my main character.

If a week has passed since the end of the story, he might still be feeling raw, nursing wounds, or the converse if things went well for him. If a decade has passed, what has he learned over those years? How has he changed? What has shifted in his perspective and understanding that he can bring to bear on his narrative?

A first person narrator who is *too* close to the events of the *now*-story is typically a poor narrator, because he can't see past the tip of his nose, so to speak. If you write a first person narrative with a character who is not able to describe events in an engaging manner, one of two things will happen: you'll have an anecdotal story with lots of "I did," "I said," or you'll create a narrative voice that is not believable when ascribed to that character. Give him enough perspective, enough scope of vision, to fulfill his narrative duties.

EXERCISE 11: DO YOU HAVE A QUALIFIED NARRATOR?

Here is a checklist you can use to assess your first person narrator. If he doesn't get high marks in all categories, you have a choice: further develop your character so he can function as the narrator, or switch to the third person, relieving him of any narrative duty.

1. In order to assess your character's narrative prowess, you need something to critique. Take out a chapter you've written in the first person. If you don't have anything written in first person, grab your journal and freewrite for fifteen minutes, using your character to tell his story. Make sure you include setting, dialogue, and action in your scene.

2. Read the scene aloud. Listen to the voice of the piece. Answer these questions:
   - How would you describe the narrative voice?
   - Does it sound like your character?
   - Does it have personality? A richness of language? Style?
   - Where in time and space is your first person narrator in relation to the *now*-story?
   - Is your first person narrator able to show?
   - Does he report events accurately in clear language?

- Unless you are writing an unreliable narrator, everything must be accurately portrayed so the reader always feels grounded within the story.
- Does your first person narrator step outside of himself to observe the scene, reflect on the action? Provide context, mood, and other narrative-enriching details that bring the scene to life for the reader?
- Is your first person narrator able to step outside of himself, but remain engaged enough to provide emotional depth in the *now*-story?
- What are your goals as a literary artist?

Now that you understand what is expected of a first person narrator, you can be sure you've made the best narrative choice for your story. Even if that choice begins with "that's how I heard the story," you'll be able to explain it to anyone who ever asks, from your mom to your thesis advisor.

KNOW THYSELF, KNOW THINE AUDIENCE

The narrator needs to have a known audience, and this is especially important with a first person narrator. You should be able to answer the question, to whom is the character telling the story?

Using first person creates a sense of familiarity between the narrator and the reader. The voice may be conversational and inviting, even chummy. "Call me Ishmael." The intimacy of first person can also feel as though the narrator is sharing a secret with you. As such, first person is well suited for stories about hidden things. In *Saving Annabelle,* Greta is telling a story of family abuse and neglect; she is at last breaking a code of silence. The narrator, however, is not telling her secret *to the reader.* For one reason, the reader does not exist in the story. For another, a story told to a general audience loses its specificity, its special intimacy. The reader should feel privileged to be hearing *this* story told in *this* way.

> In the world of your story, the reader doesn't exist, so to whom, specifically, is the story being told?

Greta tells her story to her dead sister. If she were telling the story to her parents or her minister, the tone would be dramatically different. In F. Scott Fitzgerald's *The Great Gatsby,* Nick Carraway is writing down the story of Gatsby and Daisy after some time on the East Coast, time which has disillusioned him of his great tolerance for humanity. Nick tells us he returned to the Midwest last fall, so we can suppose it is several months to a year since the events of the story. He has been grappling with the events out east for that entire time, and only now is he compelled to write it all down. Fitzgerald does not identify Nick's audience, but we might imagine he's writing the story down for therapeutic reasons, to help him make sense of everything so he can move on. This is precisely what Baz Luhrmann imagined for the 2013 film adaptation. The story is bookended by scenes of Nick in a hospital. His doctor recommends he write down his thoughts about Gatsby, suggesting Nick's audience is his doctor, and his purpose in telling this story is to facilitate his recovery.

Note that using a first person narrator allows the character to create meaning of the events for himself, as well as the audience. You should know why he is telling his story. Greta has to bring her family's secret to light so she can live without all that darkness eating her up. Nick is processing and recovering from the traumatic events out east. In the opening of the story, Nick tells us, "When I came back from the East last autumn I felt that I wanted the world to be in uniform and at a sort of moral attention forever; I wanted no more riotous excursions with privileged glimpses into the human heart."

Greta and Nick not only act in the events of the story, but they also provide the narrative exposition that surrounds the events. They must provide context, expound upon meaning, and even pass judgment. With a first person narrative, the audience cannot expect a neutral or dispassionate telling of those events. And as the writer, you must infuse your narrative with what your first person narrator needs to show his audience.

IN THE GAME OR SIDELINED?

By the time I was studying anthropology, research practices had evolved into something called "participant observation." The researcher's presence is considered enough to be a catalyst for change in the local life. While still avoiding interference, participant observation brings the anthropologist off the porch and into the community, where she can get her hands dirty.

First person narrators are the participant-observer anthropologists, fulfilling certain roles within the story. They are both acting in and observing the events of the story. That is a given.

Another given is that the narrator must be the only character who can tell this story. The reason only she can tell the story is that she is changed by the events therein. The first person narrator's life will never be the same again. That is the point of the character arc, after all.

> The first person narrator must tell the tale, because he has been changed by the events, recognizes that he has been changed, and has a need to share how he has been changed with his audience.

The first person narrator, our participant-observer, can be either the central character in the action or a peripheral character in the action. The *central first person narrator* is the clear protagonist, getting in and out of trouble, at the center of the climax. The *peripheral first person narrator* is involved in the trouble and the climax, but is telling someone else's story. Yet through this involvement and telling, he becomes a different person.

Greta is a central narrator, telling her own story. We've already discussed why she is a qualified narrator.

Nick is a peripheral narrator, telling the story of Jay Gatsby and Daisy Buchanan. Why wouldn't you want Gatsby or Daisy to tell the story? It might seem they could make the story more personal, immediate, or relevant, but not so. They lack the narrative abilities required of the first person narrator. They are self-absorbed, shortsighted, shallow, privileged, and tragic figures. At the end, Gatsby is floating in his pool. Daisy opts to remain in a loveless marriage. Nick is the one person who is profoundly changed by the story, making him the one character worthy of the mantle Point of View.

THE FIRST PERSON NARRATOR'S ARC

Narrators tell their stories from a fixed moment in time, a moment when narrator and reader converge. In a first person narrative, the character as narrator is the character *after* the events of the story have occurred. The one exception to this is, of course, a first person, present tense narrator. I'll discuss that below.

The more time your character has had to process events and gain perspective, the greater the distance from the story's events. If that chronological distance is great enough, your first person narrator can remark on events that occur after the story's end, because she will have lived beyond them. Whether the distance is short or great, your main character must be different at the end of the story than at the beginning, and your narrator will reflect that. Whether changed for the better or the worse, the narrative voice is that of the narrator (not the character), the person who has outlived the journey and has gained perspective on the past.

Besides the changes time brings to us all, like the healing of old wounds, time also brings physical, social, and philosophical changes that will be evident in your character's narrative voice. A working class kid from Boston, who grows up to be a working class man from Boston, will have a distinct voice. That voice will remain similar in region, class, and education. It will be different in experience, maturity, professional knowledge, etc.

The more your character has changed, the more changes you will need to demonstrate in your narrator's voice. If your Boston kid becomes a Harvard professor, he will belong to two worlds: his working-class roots and his intellectually refined academic profession. Both of those worlds will be woven into his narrative voice.

The differences between character and narrator are clear, exaggerated even, when the character is a child. At the opening of *Saving Annabelle*, Greta is five. At the end, she is eighteen. My narrator is also eighteen, because Greta is telling the story from the point of its close. From the first word, we clearly see the narrator is mature, knowing, and has grown up too fast. In other words, we meet Greta the first person narrator, who cannot be five, at the same time we meet Greta the character, who is five. The narrator Greta shows the reader things beyond the scope of a five-year-old that greatly enrich the story.

With a first person narrator introducing herself as a child, you can either write a juvenile narrative, suitable for young readers, or a mature narrative, suitable for adult readers. The voice of the narrator determines the presumed audience for the story. In this excerpt from *Saving Annabelle,* it is obvious that although the protagonist is a child, this is an adult story.

When Mother went into labor five weeks later, I spent the long hours that she struggled crouching in the hall, listening aghast to her moans and cries. I thought for certain Mother was being torn apart. I imagined the doctor with a saw, cutting her belly in half to extract my sisters.

The door opened at last, pulled quickly, and Doctor Bjornen stuck his head into the hallway. "Girl!" He barked the word at me as though it were a command in itself, and I responded, getting to my feet as quickly as I could on cramped legs. "Run, fetch the case on the seat of my buggy. Fast!"

I flew down the stairs and leapt from them, never touching the bottom three steps. If I were not quick enough, my mother and sisters would be lost. The doctor's phaeton was parked just in front of the house. Father had unhitched the horse and taken it to the barn to feed it, not out of consideration for the doctor, but for the beast, and because caring for the animal brought a reduction in fees. The leather seat in the buggy felt cold against my hands as I slid the large wooden box toward me. Two large crows perched in the branches of our old oak, bare but for a spattering of orange and brown leaves. The image fixed itself in my memory. I turned to go back and, in my haste, stumbled on the porch steps. The case fell from my grasp and I heard the clinking of glass bottles. Blood ran down my shin as I made my way to Mother's bedside. Presenting the box as carefully as I could in outstretched arms, I prayed that nothing inside had broken.

The distinction between the character and the narrator is clear in this passage. Greta, who is at the time of the narration a respectable young woman in Victorian Minnesota, describes herself as crouching, running, leaping, and tripping. From the physicality of the character's actions on the page, we know she is a child. Also, the doctor calls her "girl," and she jumps to action, like a child sent on a vital mission. This passage also shows Greta's powers of observation, astute memory, and ability to comment on the people around her. The child character could not accomplish all that, but the mature narrator handles her duties beautifully.

> Even with a short chronological distance between character and narrator, the narrator must be a different person than the character. This is due to the character's arc plus the narrator's hindsight.

Note: Distance is discussed fully in chapter five, "Don't Stand So Close to Me." Here we are discussing chronological distance in the first person narrative specifically. You created your own illustration of chronological distance when you did exercise four, "Understanding Narrative Distance."

I AM

The first person narrator can heighten a sense of intimacy between the reader and character. And in the present tense, the first person narrator can also create a sense of immediacy, which can heighten dramatic effect.

The risk, regardless of whether you use the past or present tense, is that the first person narrator is so engaged with the action of the story that he lacks the perspective of a true narrator. That risk is heightened in the present tense when "I felt," "I did" becomes "I feel," "I do," *because* you lose the emotional and chronological distance of a narrator who has already lived past the events of the story.

That might sound exciting and true to life, but it makes your job harder. When you write a first person, present tense narrator, you strip your narrator of perspective, growth, and hindsight. The narrator's knowledge and perspective become as limited as the character's in the *now*-story. This can have the effect of putting blinders on your narrator—which has the effect of creating an anecdotal story that is choked off by its limiting factors. This is a version of the POV stranglehold.

Here is an example of a first person, present tense narrator that illustrates the myopic scope often encountered with an underqualified narrator.

I look at the pie on the plate. It's blueberry. I don't even like blueberries, but when it was offered to me, I didn't know how to refuse. Now here I am with a plate full of blueberry pie in front of me. *How did I get here?* I wonder.

Jim comes over to sit next to me. He slaps me on the back just as I'm taking a sip of coffee. The coffee sloshes out of the cup and splashes onto the pie. Maybe it will be an improvement.

"What's new?" Jim says. He's wearing a plaid flannel shirt.

"I hate blueberries."

He nods toward the plate on the counter, his eyebrows raised.

"I couldn't say no."

CHAPTER 11: IT'S MINE, ALL MINE

He hooks the lip of the plate with his finger and slides it over in front of him. "Problem solved."

I wish I could give Jim all of my problems.

The scope of the story presented to the reader is very small. It's as though the story is contained in the narrator's bubble of personal space, with a radius of about three feet in any direction from the narrator himself. The rest of the world does not exist. We have no sense of place or time. We are left to surmise that he is sitting in a diner, but couldn't he be sitting in a kitchen with a breakfast bar? Eventually, he uses the word "counter," but if he's at the counter, what about the people behind it? The waitstaff? The window to the kitchen across from him? The sounds of cooking and eating all around? Or is this diner empty but for him and the mystery character who served the pie? Where did Jim come from? Outside? Another table? From behind the cash register? We have no idea, because the narrative scope is constricted to only what is right before our nameless narrator.

The narrator and his friend Jim are faceless blobs. All we can say for certain about them is that Jim wears plaid flannel. Maybe he's a trucker. Maybe he's a financier on a fly fishing vacation. We can't tell, because he is so nondescript. And what do we really know about our narrator? The narrator could easily be a woman, for all we know. Perhaps he or she will go to the restroom after drinking that coffee and take a look at the symbol on the door. When a first person narrator is so stingy with the details, readers are left waiting and wondering until some clue pops into the scene. Narrators like this one are not qualified to bring us into a world that exists outside of their own heads.

Your job is to bring the world you envision to life on the page and invite your readers to enter it and enjoy their visit. If your readers aren't tempted to write postcards home, you may need a new narrator.

Let's look at an excerpt in the first person, present tense point of view that works. This narrator does her job well. This is from one of my short stories, "Delilah." It has already been established that Delilah, the narrator, and Sammie, her best friend, work in a beauty salon in a small town.

The Cut N Blow is dead, the last of the appointments took care of and out the door. While I sweep up, Sammie dozes in one of the chairs that backs up to the washing station, her neck cradled by the padded sink. Guess she and Tom had a late night, because her mouth hangs partly open and she's making a wheezy sound lying all tipped back like that. After sweeping, I restock the bottles of Luscious Shampoo and watch her sleep.

I pick up my sheers and walk over to Sammie.

I gently stroke Sammie's head, lifting and dropping her hair, just like I would if I was about to wash it. When Sammie doesn't wake, I lift a section of hair and cut it off, right at the center of her forehead. No fix could blend that into a hairdo. I find myself grinning. It isn't a full smile, it isn't happiness, but it's some kind of glee. I felt this once as a girl, when I told

Carly to hand over her roller skates, and she did. Just like that. I work quickly, snipping away one chunk of hair after another, close to the scalp. I'm careful around the ears. At the back of the head, I have to reach into the sink basin and work by feel. I stuff handfuls of hair into the pocket of my plastic apron. When I'm done, I'm practically giggling, and I would have bust a gut if Sammie weren't asleep, muttering as her hair is stripped from her head.

I get out of there as soon as I'm done, holding the tattle bells as I softly close the door.

In the car, with the windows down, I let myself laugh out loud. I've always loved the wind on my face, in my hair. I race past low rows of soybeans and hold my arm out the window, releasing fistfuls of long, dark curls. The strands separate on the wind. Some lift, floating out over the fields, like dancing curlicues. Others fall to the earth quickly, wrapping themselves in the weedy plants that grow in the margins between field and road. As the high sun catches the hairs, they look brown, burgundy, and black in turns. A crow joins the dance in the wind and catches some strands of hair in his beak, mid-flight.

Unlike the narrator in the diner, Delilah describes her movements through the setting, her actions, her friend, her thoughts and feelings, and a tableau of the hair and crow dancing over a field of soybeans. The goal is not to create an exhaustive list of visuals or the character's feelings, but to give enough detail to actively engage the reader's imagination, so that he feels like he's participating in the narrator's story. To do this, your narrator needs to be present to the world around her.

EXERCISE 12: WORKING FIRST PERSON

For this exercise, you're going to work with the same point of view character from the "Working Third Person" exercise in chapter eight, "He Said, She Said." But do not read that scene. You need to start fresh, because the many intricacies of each point of view will shape a completely different narrative.

1. Have your main character in mind. Now let's put him into conflict: he just got caught with his hand in the cookie jar. Use the same scenario as before, the same characters. If the cookie jar involved your character stealing his teacher's grade book to doctor his grades, that's what he'll do in this scene.

2. Write in the first person, past tense point of view, with a central narrator.

3. Make certain your narrator has a strong presence on the page. Describe. Expound. Reflect. Show.

    Do not write a scene that is entirely dialogue and characters moving around the stage of the page. Flex some narrative muscles. Think about the mood of the scene and how you want your readers to feel about the character and his world.

4. Open your journal and get your pencil ready. Set a timer for fifteen minutes. Ready? Go!

5. Stop when the timer goes off. If you have a page of "I don't know what to write," try again. Otherwise, read it. Do not worry about whether or not it's good.

6. Answer the following questions in your journal:

    – Is the character as narrator's voice distinct from the character as actor's voice? How so?

    – What is the mood of the scene? How has the narrative voice established the mood?

    – What is the chronological and emotional distance between the character as narrator and character as actor? How does your choice about the chronological and emotional distance shape what is on the page? If he is in his seat in detention describing how he got busted, things will be pretty raw. If he's a father telling his son about that time long ago, he'll have a different take on the events.

    – What has the narrator shown the reader and how might it affect the reader? Has the narrator shown things the actor might not know in the moment, thanks to his perspective, hindsight, and powers of perception?

    – Overall, what are your impressions of this scene? What are the effects of the choices you made?

    – Was it easy or difficult to write? Why? How? What did you learn from this exercise?

EXERCISE 13: ON THE ONE HAND AND ON THE OTHER

In this exercise, you will compare your third and first person narratives.

- Read both scenes side by side and answer these questions in your journal:
  - How are they different?
  - What effect do the two points of view have on you as a reader?
  - Did the emotional and/or psychic distance change? Were you trying to change it, or was it a result of the shift in point of view?
  - Which point of view works better here and might be better overall for this character and this story? Why?
  - Which point of view felt more natural to write? Which one was more challenging? Why?
  - What did you learn from doing this exercise?

Note that your answer here only applies to these two scenes. It is not an absolute about the power of third or first person points of view.

You can repeat this exercise as often as you like. In fact, it can be useful to do whenever you begin a new book project. Write the first chapter in different points of view to see which is more powerful. Try a different character for the point of view. Try to get emotionally close and emotionally distant. Experiment and play.

The best point of view for the story might not be the one you're most comfortable writing. It is the point of view that tells the story in the best way possible.

RECAP

In this chapter, we examined the strengths and weaknesses of the first person narrator.

- First person narratives can be intimate, but are not necessarily closer than a third person narrative. In fact, a close, third person narrative should be as subjective and as intimate as a first person narrative.
- Writing a first person narrative can lull you into complacency, believing you have done your authorial job because you have written something diary-like.
- A first person narrative is a good way to craft your story when your narrator is uniquely qualified to tell the story herself.
- Your first person narrator must use language well, be a great observer, report things accurately, know how to *show*, separate herself as narrator from herself as actor, and own her story.
- Exercise 11: Do You Have a Qualified Narrator? In this exercise, you assessed a scene you wrote in the first person to see if your narrator qualifies for the job.

- Your first person narrator should have a specific audience for his story.

- Your first person narrator will be either central or peripheral to the action.

- Your first person narrator is a different person than the actor, due to the changes created over the character arc plus the passage of time, and development of hindsight.

- The first person, present tense point of view can seem immediate, or it can create a myopic perspective that does the story and reader a disservice.

- Exercise 12: Working First Person. In this exercise, you rewrote the scene from the "Working Third Person" exercise, this time using a first person, past tense, central narrator.

- Exercise 13: On the One Hand and On the Other. In this exercise, you compared your scenes from the exercises "Working Third Person" and "Working First Person."

Chapter 12

"Trust Me"

YOU CAN'T TRUST ME

As a reader, you put yourself in the hands of the narrator, who is assumed competent and trustworthy. Most of the time, he is. But every once in a while you encounter an unreliable narrator, a storyteller who lures you in and then shakes you up, causing you to doubt everything you thought you knew about this story's world.

If it's done well, you enjoy the doubt and suspicion caused by this unreliable narrator. If it's not done well, the doubt turns to frustration and the suspicion to confusion. How long will you put up with frustration and confusion? I'm betting, not long.

As a writer, why risk losing your readers to a narrator they can't trust?

The first, obvious answer is your story might best be told by an unreliable narrator, one who is going to twist and warp the truth as it's presented to the reader. Or you might be interested in the destabilizing effects the reader will feel when she realizes the story is laced with lies. You might be tempted by the challenge of crafting a tightly woven narrative that holds together despite its fallacies. And it's fun to write the unreliable narrator. In other words, your reasons for writing an unreliable narrator come down to

- craft and the story's structure,
- audience and the effect you want the point of view to have on the reader, and
- creative process and artistry.

LIAR, LIAR, PANTS ON FIRE!

An *unreliable narrator* is one who lies to the reader. If your narrator is only lying to other characters, it doesn't count. If he lies and then admits it or corrects himself, it doesn't count. The key to the unreliable narrative is that the reader believes something, which later is revealed to be untrue, forcing the reader to reconsider her relationship to the characters and the story.

The unreliable narrator is one whose veracity, motives, and character are brought into question through inconsistencies in the point of view, through one or more characters' perspectives. The resulting effect upon the reader is destabilizing, precisely because she can't bring herself to trust him.

A narrator might lie for the same reasons any of us might: guilt, shame, manipulation, greed, mental illness, memory loss, head trauma, unbearable grief, fun and games, ignorance of the truth... A reader will tolerate the unreliable narrator because it's fun to solve a riddle and it's fun to be surprised. Keep in mind that truth and lies have much to do with the perspective through which we experience an event. Facts are objective and provable. The truth is often subjective and malleable.

TWISTING THE TRUTH IN FIRST AND THIRD

We might be tempted to think unreliable narrators are only found in first person narratives. It is easiest to conceive of the lying liar as a character, one who is other than the authorial voice, walking and talking on the stage of the page, distinct from the author and so, in a way, keeping the writer's hands clean. But you can write a close, third person unreliable narrator just as easily.

How is this? Did I not say that the authorial narrator is reliable? Yes, but...

The traditional authorial-omniscient narrator is reliable. However, the close, third person narrator is another persona of the author, one who is as subjective as the first person narrator. She may read as dispassionate and neutral as any other authorial narrator, but she is so deeply enmeshed in the point of view character's perspective that the story is practically a first person narrative.

Thus, the writer has two choices when creating an unreliable narrator: first person or close third. The key in a close, third person point of view is to keep the narrative lens as tightly confined by the worldview, insights, and experiences of the point of view character as you would in a first person point of view. The psychic distance is kept very close throughout the story, because it is through this unreliable *perspective* that the narrative functions to deceive the reader.

Let's consider some examples of unreliable narrators.

Stephen King's novella, *Secret Window, Secret Garden,* provides an example of an unreliable narrator told in the close, third person point of view. Mort Rainey is a writer who has been traumatized by discovering that his wife cheated on him and by their ensuing divorce. A strange man called Shooter turns up at his lake cabin to accuse him of stealing a short story. Shooter then begins a reign of psychological terror. The twist at the end of the story is that Mort and Shooter are the same person. The use of a close, third person point of view presents Shooter and all the events of the story to the reader through Mort's eyes. Beyond that, it is Mort's *mind* that is coping with each turn of events, influencing the reader's interpretation of those events. Very early in the story, Mort hears Shooter's voice—his diction, his accent—in his mind. We assume naturally that Mort is using his memory to make this imagined threat sound more ominous. Post-reveal, however, we are invited to change our opinion of what that moment means: the voice wasn't imagined. It was really Shooter speaking to Mort from inside his own head, because Shooter is an aspect of Mort.

When a story's big reveal confirms our narrator is unreliable, we are invited to re-examine our relationship to the entire story and its characters. That is the fun of reading a story with an unreliable narrator. Just as it's fun to try to solve a mystery before the detective, and to piece everything together at the end, it is fun to think over the unreliable narrative just read to see what clues the writer put in place for the reader. That voice in Mort's head, were you clever enough to think it was more than his imagination? When did you start seeing the similarities between Mort and Shooter as more than coincidence?

Chuck Palahniuk's *Fight Club* opens with the unnamed first person narrator standing with a gun in his mouth held by one Tyler Durden. Naturally, the reader pictures two men. In the first couple of pages, the narrator says that he knows how to make bombs because Tyler knows how. The reader assumes, of course, this is because Tyler instructed the narrator at some point before this moment in time. The twist is that the narrator and Tyler are the same person. At the end of the book, the story comes back around to that opening scene. Now the narrator is free, post-reveal, to tell us directly that to an observer, there is one man holding a gun in his own mouth, but really, there are two men here, him and Tyler. *Really,* because for the narrator and the reader who has been a passenger on the narrator's ride, there are two men in the scene.

In *The Story Works Guide to Writing Character*, I discussed Dennis Lehane's *Shutter Island* as an example of an unreliable narrator. It is also a close, third person point of view. You can find that discussion in *Character's* chapter ten, "The Big Uns."

THERE'S HIS STORY, THERE'S HER STORY, AND THERE'S THE TRUTH

Another way to create an unreliable narrator is to use two characters' perspectives that create doubt about one another.

In Gillian Flynn's *Gone Girl*, we encounter two point of view characters who alternate chapters. Nick Dunne tells the *now*-story when his wife goes missing from their home with signs of a struggle. His wife, Amy, provides the backstory to their relationship through diary entries in part one of the book. She is missing both from their home and from the present-day story, but her diary provides the reader with a record of her life with Nick that informs the reader's opinion of Nick and everything he professes in his narrative. With only Nick's story, the reader has no reason to doubt him. His explanations and excuses for certain questionable behaviors would be relatable, and the reader would likely give him a pass. After all, his wife just went missing; how is he supposed to behave? When also seen through Amy's eyes, however, Nick becomes dubious.

As the reader gets deeper into the story, she has to wonder if Nick is lying or if his subjective version of the truth is simply different from Amy's subjective version of the truth. A major twist occurs around the midpoint. In part two, it is revealed that Amy fakes her own death. Her chapters are no longer the diary entries of a victim, but the *now*-story narrative of a woman who fakes her death and frames her husband for murder. The reader had no reason to doubt the veracity of the diary, so the twist comes as a shocking reveal that turns upside down everything she thought about both Nick and Amy.

Let's look at how two unreliable narrators present the same story in a classic case of "he said, she said." The scenes below are from my third Skoghall Mystery, *Don't Get Stuck in Skoghall*.

She screamed at him. She was always screaming at him lately. "So what is she to you? Just another mid-life crisis, I suppose."

"More like a mid-life *wake up call*," Dick shot back. "I'm through, Carole." God, it felt good to say it. He'd been so afraid to tell her how he really felt. Well, not really that, the telling, but the repercussions that were sure to follow. Divorce. She'd make sure it got ugly. They'd have to liquidate property. She'd expect alimony for the rest of her life—good God. Dick rolled his eyes at the thought. He'd need another attorney now. Dick began running through his list of contacts, noting those who were in a position to recommend one. Despite all these new complications, he felt free for the first time in years. Big snowflakes twirled and danced as they made their descent to earth. A sign from Heaven that everything would be all right for Dick.

"What do you mean you're through?" Her voice went shrill whenever she got upset. It was a sound that had aggravated Dick for half of his life.

"Through. Done. Finished." Carole's cheeks had reddened in the cold. No wonder. She drove out from the Cities in a fashionable, unlined, short-waisted wool jacket with autumnal leaves embroidered on the lapels and cuffs. Was it embroidery? Or appliqué? Dick could never keep that sort of thing straight. It mattered to Carole, and if he got it wrong, if he called embroidery appliqué, she corrected him like he was some kind of moron.

They stood on the edge of a storm. A great big beautiful winter storm, the likes of which the region hadn't seen in over five years, not since global warming made the Upper Midwest a temperate climate. Sixty degrees in November. Preposterous. And more than disappointing: disastrous. When folks as far north as Ely had to truck up to Canada to play in the snow, economies collapsed. Here it was Thanksgiving weekend and Dick had something to be grateful for.

"What are we doing here, Dickie?" Carole gestured, raising her hands to her sides like maybe he could explain it.

"You drove, Carole. Hell if I know what we're doing here."

Carole had arrived at the bluff house earlier than anticipated, and Dick hadn't finished cleaning up. When she saw the wineglass with the lipstick print on the rim, she snatched it up and threw it at him. It was so obvious, maybe he wanted to be caught after all. She fled the cabin, and Dick followed her like a fool. Hadn't twenty-seven years of marriage taught him anything? This wasn't her usual fly-off-the-handle dramatics. She had proof, albeit shattered on the floor. That's why he followed her out to the car, left the front door open, the fire in the fireplace roaring, and jumped in the passenger side as she backed out. He'd never expected her to leave the driveway.

But she did. She sped down the bluff and raced up the River Road with Dick white-knuckled, doing his own screaming in the passenger seat. She'd always preferred washable mascara. Lit by the dashboard lights, she looked like a ghoulish raccoon, while the first fat snowflakes appeared in the headlights. She turned hard onto Skoghall's Main Street and screeched to a stop beside the community garden. She jumped out of the car and rushed into the dark enclave of dormant flowerbeds and leafless trees. Dick chased her to the dead end, here on the footbridge over the spring. A light above the café's door lit them under the dazzling winter sky.

"Carole," he said, holding his hand out, palm up, "when's the last time you caught a snowflake on your hand and looked at it?"

"What?" she spat out the word. "Dickie, you're a ridiculous man."

"Look." He lowered his hand and pointed at a perfectly shaped snowflake resting on the pad below his middle finger. "See the prongs? The structure? Right there, you can see it with the naked eye."

"I'll give you naked," she muttered.

"Snow has been like miniature chips of ice lately, like hard, jagged lumps of stuff. But this..." He raised his hand closer to Carole's face. "This is perfect. It's like the snow we grew up with. A real flake."

"You're a flake." Carole pressed her thumb to Dick's hand, melting the snowflake. "You cheated on me, Dickie. And now you tell me you're through." She sniffled, but was it a show of emotion, or just the cold making her nose run?

The snow was coming harder now and would be piling up. With the temperature dropping, the roads would freeze and the lakes would follow. The region had thrived for more than a hundred years because of winter tourism, winter sports, and Dick's grandfather had capitalized on the move away from shacks constructed with scrap lumber and old doors to slick, prefabricated models with added comforts. "Even on the bitterest of winter days, you'll sit pretty in a Pratney Ice House." Pratney Ice House, Inc. was in the red for the third year in a row, and this storm, it might as well have been dropping flakes of gold.

"Come on, Carole. Let's go back to the house. We'll have some brandy and talk this through."

"But..." she sniffled again, "you want a divorce?"

"Don't you?"

"No." Carole had brought her purse out of the car with her. Dick hadn't really noticed it. It didn't even make sense for her to have it, other than force of habit. He noticed it now as she reached her right hand across her body to grab the handles and swing it upward with the full force of both of her arms. She put her shoulders into it and rotated at the waist. Her golfing coach would be pleased. The bag, a $2600 Prada tote in caramel, made of calf leather in Italy, with a flat bottom fitted with brass feet to keep it off the floor, something Dick had always teased her about, calling it her luggage, arced upward from Carole's hip toward his chest. The hard bottom caught him squarely in the sternum. He rocked onto his heels and flailed his arms. The bag caught him under the chin next and knocked him backwards. Dick felt the footbridge's railing pressing into his back. He grabbed for it. Snow made the wooden handrail slick, hard to grasp. And then the bag came down from above and slammed into his face, the straight edge of that bottom cracking the bridge of his nose. He bent over the railing in a way he never would have imagined his body could bend. His feet slid out from under him and he flipped backwards.

The fall covered a short distance, not even enough time to grasp what was happening. His backside hit the water first and his head struck a weathered paddle of the waterwheel. A bit of hair and scalp came free, stuck to a splintering of the board. The cold of the water caused him to gasp for air—a reflex, one he knew the dangers of, being an ice fisherman, but one he had not trained to prevent in the recent years of mild winters and warm lakes. If he had not struck his head… Or if he had not gasped for air as he sank into the spring, filling his lungs with icy water…

Carole leaned over the railing, her hands gripping the soft leather of her purse's double handles. She had to stand on tiptoe to look down at the dark spring that had so quickly taken her husband. "I want…" she paused to catch her breath, to watch the fresh snowflakes already cover the handrail where Dickie had tried to stop his fall, "you to die and make me a rich widow."

What do you understand to have happened in this scene? How do you feel about these characters? Do you align yourself with one of them more than the other? Let's see what happened from Carole's perspective. We'll pick up the scene when Carole stops the car on Skoghall's Main Street.

Carole looked over at her husband and was overwhelmed by the urge to get away from him.

She climbed out on unstable legs, pushed her door shut with both hands, and stayed there, palms on the cold frame of her car. The street was dark, silent. She realized they were on Skoghall's little hill of a Main Street. A dozen or so shops, all tourist season stuff. All closed for the winter. Carole opened the back seat door and grabbed her handbag, a tote Dick liked to call her luggage. *Ha. Ha.* She turned around, pressed herself against the car just to feel something solid behind her, then she walked away. Carole left Dick in the car and went into the community garden, her feet carrying her into a sanctuary. *A hush fell over the garden,* she thought as the snow fell faster and heavier, collecting in the bends and creases of dead plants. On any other occasion, Carole would have mentally scolded the shopkeepers of Skoghall for not properly clearing their garden for winter.

When she reached the bridge over the spring, there was nowhere to go except around and back to the car, back to

Dick. So she stood under the café's porch light. The rage of earlier had laid down, temporarily exhausted, like an abused dog that had spent the last hour snapping and barking at the end of its chain. It would come back. Carole knew that and counted on it. Her rage had been her ally on more than one occasion. Righteous indignation looks pretty, she liked to say to her girlfriend-du-jour whenever telling one of her "so I got mad" stories, but if you want results, you have to *rage*. "Get mad like a man, honey," she'd end her parable—always told for the benefit of her friend-in-need, not for self-gratification—with that line and a pat on the knee. There would be time enough to get mad. Right now, Carole wanted to feel hurt. She wanted to curl up in the pain of a discovered betrayal and hide her face. Pain could be satisfying in its own way.

Carole heard the car door open and close, loud and intrusive in this sleeping garden. She breathed deeply while she waited for Dick to arrive on the bridge beside her. Three... Inhale, letting the abdomen expand. Exhale, relaxing her shoulders. A counselor had taught her this a decade ago when all she really wanted out of the session was a prescription. Five... Six...

"Carole." Dick wore a t-shirt and lounge pants. He'd slipped his running shoes on, no socks. He'd be freezing soon.

"How could you do that to me, Dick? All the lies you must have told." She shook her head sadly. The other woman would be younger than her. They always were. She would be thinner and fitter, without the worry lines between her brows, without the laugh lines at the corners of her eyes. Dick had kept his hair on his head and fat off his belly. His father had been lean his entire life. Carole used to think that boded well for her. She turned away from him and looked into the garden, the café's light at her back.

"What the hell did you think you were doing? Driving like that. You could have killed us both. We're goddam lucky you didn't crash the Mercedes."

Carole pressed a hand to her forehead. "I don't know, Dickie. I was...*am*. I am distraught." She faced him, looked into his eyes. "I was so mad when I found the room like that, but now..."

"Now what, Carole?" Dick had never been patient when she tried to express her deeper feelings. She supposed it was why she let herself react to things, and often badly. If he was going to bark at her while she tried to find the words to express how she really felt, what she really needed, why bother? It became easier after a few years of marriage to simply unleash her emotions. Subtlety was lost on Dick; he understood big. So each tiff became a storm. A mistress, though. This was no tiff. It would not and could not blow over. A mistress. *This* was a tornado.

"Let me think! Dick, you don't let me think. You make demands while I'm trying to sort things out. Give me a minute."

"Give you a minute? We're standing outside in a snowstorm, Carole." Dick shivered as though on cue, and the snow gathering on the top of his head and shoulders trembled.

"Give me the keys. I'll drive us home and you can have your minute there."

"Home? To Minneapolis?"

"Don't be stupid. That's over an hour away. We'll go back to the bluff house."

"How could you do it? Did you get bored? Are you tired of me?" Snowflakes landed on Carole's face and melted, leaving her cheeks glistening with moisture. One caught on the prongs of her eyelashes and she left it there to become liquid. Dick snatched at Carole's jacket, and she pulled away. "What are you doing?"

"The keys, Carole. They're in your pocket, aren't they?" He snatched at her again, grabbing the hem of her jacket and yanking her toward him. One hand held the jacket, crumpling the suede in a tight fist. The other hand reached into the slash pocket and yanked out her keys.

He released her and held the keys up, the ring looped over one finger, and jangled them in her face. Carole had both hands on the calfskin handles of her tote and she swung it, arcing from her hips, upward across her body. She put her shoulders into it, rotated her torso to follow through—her golfing coach had not been a waste of time after all—and the corner of the square-bottomed handbag caught Dick in the sternum, then under the chin. He stumbled backwards, put his hands out for balance, and dropped the keys on the bridge. He bent backwards over the railing and his feet flew up. Carole tried to grab an ankle, a pant leg, but it was so quick, back and over. Just like that. She heard a thud and then the slap of a body hitting water.

Carole cried out her husband's name, rushed to the railing and leaned over it. She stretched her hand to the spring below, ready to catch Dick when he emerged with a great gasp. He would climb out, coughing water, doubled over and shivering. She would help him to the car, wrap him in the wool blanket she put in her trunk at the start of every winter with her emergency flares, energy bars, and bottled water.

"Dickie?"

The water, black and cold, offered her no sign her husband had ever existed.

Carole turned and shook the café's door. She spun around to face the buildings that surrounded the garden, then looked at the street and the buildings across it. All dark. All still. Skoghall had closed for the winter.

She picked up the keys, looked at the spring again, saw nothing again, and hurried back to the car. Her phone had been dead before she left home, so she put it on the charger in the car. She got in the car, picked up her phone, pressed the power button.

Nothing.

She pressed it again and held it for a full five seconds. Nothing.

She lifted the phone away from the center console and the cable came with it, the USB end dangling free.

Carole pressed her brow to the steering wheel between both hands and squeezed her eyes shut. *Oh God. Oh God. Oh God. What do I do?* In response to her question, she remembered something useful. Her father had taught her two things. One, when you don't know what to do, look to the facts. Two, if all else fails, go home and see what tomorrow brings.

Fact: Dick was gone.

Fact: Dick cheated on her.

Fact: She wasn't supposed to be here until tomorrow.

And: She could go home. She could go home and see what tomorrow brings.

What do you understand to have happened in this scene? How do you feel about these characters now? Did your allegiance change?

If I only presented one perspective, the reader would accept it as the truth. And it would be—it is the truth of the character whose perspective is the reader's vehicle through this story. By presenting the reader with two versions of the scene, I create room for doubt and speculation about both characters, their actions, and their motives. What really happened? I'm not going to say.

ANOTHER OPTION?

Could you have an unreliable narrator who is not relating the first person or close, third person point of view character's experience? Yes. You could create a character-narrator the reader is aware of, but who is not part of the story or is only peripherally in the story.

Such a device typically employs framing. The reader would meet the character-narrator at the beginning and end of the story, though during the story he could disappear, reading just like an authorial narrator. The writer could, if desired, occasionally remind the reader of who the narrator is, interjecting brief glimpses of the character-narrator, possibly framing the breaks between each act, or using phrases like "my father" to signal the narrator's relationship to the story.

Suppose this character is telling the story of his father's heroic deeds during a great war. The main character is the father. The setting is the battlefield. The child is back home and has no way of knowing what the father is really doing during this time. Perhaps the narrator tells the reader what he was told about or by his father. Perhaps it is all an invention, what he wishes is true. When the reveal comes, we learn that the father is a coward or a criminal.

This character-narrator might be ignorant of the truth and the reveal could be as much of a shock to him as to the reader. Or he might be so ashamed of the truth that lying about his father is a coping mechanism. If he is ignorant of the truth, the reader might sympathize with him when the reveal is made. He would be a victim of deceit. And if he knows what his father did, but is consciously lying to the reader, he may be pathetic but not sympathetic as a perpetrator of those lies. His motivation would probably determine the readers' final judgment.

This character-narrator would function similarly to the peripheral first person narrator in that he is telling someone else's story. He would, however, be outside the main story, existing in a space off the stage of the page.

TIME TO REVEAL THE TRUTH

When working with any unreliable narrator, you are essentially constructing a mystery, presenting one version of events through the lying narrator, and holding back another version of events. This requires careful plotting. You'll have to keep track of two stories as you write, the truth and the lie, or version A and version B. You'll have to skillfully manage the narrative, building intrigue and avoiding confusion. An unreliable narrative begs the question, "What really happened?" If you give the reader clues along the way, creating a sense that things are not as they seem, he'll begin his own detective work as he reads, looking for the truth between the lines. That second, true version of the story comes out, like the whodunit at the end of a mystery, when it is time for your big reveal.

The reveal typically occurs at the end of act two. It is the event that catapults the protagonist toward the inevitable climax. After the reveal, the climax takes on a previously unexpected shape because of the revelation just made by both the protagonist and the reader.

This reveal can set everything right, telling the reader **the whole truth**, which gives her the opportunity to revise her understanding of the story. Or the reveal can lead to an **ambiguous ending**, one in which the reader knows she's been lied to, but the facts are left uncertain and open to interpretation.

The reveal could take the form of a **twist**, a shock for the reader in which the plot is turned around, as in a reversal of fortune or consequences. What the reader thought she knew is suddenly given new meaning. If a narrator is revealed to be unreliable only at the end of the story, in a sudden and dramatic twist, the reader would likely not see it coming because any clues provided are subtle and meant to be recognized only in hindsight.

The reveal could also come not as a shock to the reader, but as a **solution to the riddle** created by the unsettling aspects of the narrative. With this kind of reveal, the writer has provided clues in the form of inconsistencies throughout the story, so that the reader becomes suspicious of the narrator and his motives for telling this story. Ideally, the reader becomes curious about the truth and engages with these clues, trying to decipher the real story within the one being told. The reveal may prove the reader's assumptions right or wrong, but should satisfy the reader with some combination of inevitability, plausibility, and surprise.

Once the reader is in on the deception, she should be able to identify inconsistencies in the narrative, if only in hindsight. Those inconsistencies function as clues that the narrator is unreliable and there is more to the story than he is letting on.

EXERCISE 14: THE FLIMFLAM MAN, WOMAN, AND COUPLE

If you've already worked through the exercises in *The Story Works Guide to Writing Character*, you've already done part one of this exercise. I'm reprinting it here because you might not have seen it before. And if you've done this one before, go ahead and do it again. See what else you can come up with. New day. New unreliable narrator.

In part two of this exercise, you're going to build on part one by freewriting.

Part One

This will help you decide if an unreliable narrator is going to work for your story.

1. How is an unreliable narrator essential to your story?
2. Answer some questions about your narrator.
    –   What does the narrator have to hide?
    –   Is the narrator lying to himself, as well as the reader?
    –   Why is the narrator compelled to lie?
    –   What does he gain?
        How will those lies fit into your plot? Consider their purpose in the story and what clues you'll leave the reader along the way.
        How will your character's lies affect other characters? Will you leave the reader uncertain at the end of the book or include a reveal in which all is made clear? Why?

Part Two

Now that you know why you need an unreliable narrator, what effect this will have on your story and your readers, as well as how it's all going to end, it's time to get writing.

1. Grab your journal and pencil. Put your point of view character in a situation in which he has something to hide from the reader.

    -   To whom is the story being told? Your narrator has something to hide, so whom is he hiding it from?

    -   Is the character willfully deceiving the reader? Why or why not? You need to understand his motive to deceive in order to select what to put on the page.

    -   What clues can you include in the narrative to indicate that this story is not exactly true? In the discussion of King's *Secret Window, Secret Garden* and Palahniuk's *Fight Club*, I noted that both stories plant clues in early pages: Shooter's voice in Mort's head and the narrator knows something because Tyler knows it, respectively. Clues that when initially read are taken at face value, but take on new meaning after the reveal.

2. Set your timer for fifteen minutes. Ready? Go!

3. Read over what you wrote.

    -   How did you incorporate deception into the narrative? On the surface, everything should be believable, but some detail you included is intended to make the reader uneasy, if only subconsciously, and in hindsight those discrepancies or deceits will be made clear.

    -   What is going to keep a reader interested in your unreliable narrator? Often these troubled characters are less than completely likable. Dick is having an affair. Carole seems rather hysterical and vengeful. When you decrease the likable factor, you must increase the fascinating factor. With unreliable narrators, the mystery around "What really happened?" will contribute to the fascination factor. Flynn's Amy is the paragon of the likable character in part one of *Gone Girl*, while post-reveal she's hateful but fascinating.

- What is the truth? The real truth, not your narrator's subjective truth. At some point in the story, you'll have to reveal the truth to the reader. This typically occurs at the end of act two, setting up the climax, as in King's and Palahniuk's stories. As we saw in Flynn's *Gone Girl,* however, the twist could occur at the midpoint—provided the rest of the story is equally engaging without the deception.

If answering these questions makes the way to writing your story seem muddy instead of clear, reconsider using an unreliable narrator. If, on the other hand, your answers have motivated you to get writing, get writing!

RECAP

In this chapter, we examined the unreliable narrator and what kind of a game he (*you*) is playing with the reader.

- Unreliable narrators add layers of complexity to a story.
- The unreliable narrator is one whose veracity, motives, and character are brought into question through inconsistencies in

the narrative, through one or more characters' perspectives. The resulting effect upon the reader is destabilizing, precisely because she can't bring herself to trust him.

- An unreliable narrator requires careful plotting. You'll have to keep track of two stories as you write and carefully manage the narrative.

- Unreliable narrators might lie for the same reasons you or I might lie, from ignorance to mental illness.

- Your unreliable narrator is most often a first person or close third point of view character.

- You can use two point of view characters' perspectives to create doubt about each other's versions of what happened.

- You could also write a character-storyteller as the unreliable narrator who is telling a story about a protagonist.

- Your unreliable narrator is constructing a mystery around the question, "What really happened?"

- The big reveal most often occurs at the end of act two, setting up the climax of the story.

- The reveal may tell the whole truth, lead to an ambiguous ending, take the form of a twist, or finally solve a riddle.

- Once the reveal has occurred and the reader is aware of the deception, she should be able to review the story and find clues you've laced throughout the narrative.

- Exercise 14: The Flimflam Man, Woman, and Couple. In this exercise, you answered some questions about the possible role of an unreliable narrator in your story. Then you freewrote a scene in which your narrator lies to your reader.

Chapter 13

Earning Their Keep

ONLY SOME GET TO WEAR THE CROWN

You've seen many wrong turns along Point of View Lane: head hopping, reduced tension, spoiled reveals, unqualified narrators, poorly defined protagonists, and more. The worst wrong turn of all is the unearned point of view, but what does it mean to have an earned point of view? What should you do when you find yourself tempted to create a new point of view character for the sake of the reader? And how do you make sure all of your point of view characters have earned their starring roles in your story?

> If you have a point of view character who has not earned the title, "Off with her head!"

EARNING POINTS

Let's summarize what we've learned about qualifying for the role of point of view character. To earn a point of view:

- A character has to bring a perspective to bear on the story in a unique and interesting way.
- She has to be the one with the most to gain or lose from the events of the story.
- In the case of multiple perspectives, each point of view character must face significant gains and losses.
- He must not clutter, confuse, or distract from the story in any way.
- She must never reduce tension or spoil reveals.

In chapter eleven, "It's Mine, All Mine," I noted that Nick Carraway, the narrator of F. Scott Fitzgerald's *The Great Gatsby,* is changed by the events of the story. Here, it doesn't matter that Nick is a first person narrator. We're not looking at his qualifications to narrate. We're examining whether Nick is even an effective point of view character. He's good for this because, at first glance, he does not seem to conform to the criteria above. Let's see how he actually measures up.

- Is the perspective Nick brings to the story unique and interesting?

Nick is a witness, sharing Gatsby and Daisy's story with the world. As such, he is in a position to comment on their lifestyle and choices, the beauty and sloth of extreme affluence, the recklessness and greed of a certain class of people at a certain time in history. Nick does not belong to their class; he has an in because he is Daisy's cousin. As such, he makes observations Gatsby and Daisy would never be able to make. So, yes, his perspective is unique and interesting.

- Does Nick have the most to gain or lose from the story?

It may not seem that way initially. After all, he's a witness. It is not his heart on the line, his life that stands to change if Gatsby gets the girl. But Gatsby ends up getting shot over a crime he didn't commit, and Daisy and Tom move away from Long Island. If you examine their character arcs, Gatsby spends the entire novel in pursuit of one goal. When he gets what he wants, everything goes sideways, and he's killed. Daisy has the opportunity to change, but goes back to her husband. Nick, however, has been affected by the events of the story and will never be quite the same person again. Therefore, yes, he has the most to gain or lose. Remember, gains and losses are not necessarily material.

- Does Nick's point of view clutter, confuse, or distract from the story in any way?

He is a reliable narrator who is everywhere he needs to be to bring the story to the reader. He is the only point of view. As a participant and an observer, he is well-placed to tell the story while exploring its meaning and providing social commentary. He is a first person narrator with the emotional and chronological distance required to tell the story. No, he does not clutter, confuse, or distract from the story.

- Does Nick ever reduce the tension or spoil reveals?

His distance from the other characters helps to create tension and timely reveals. The reader learns things as Nick does. For example, the mysterious Jay Gatsby remains mysterious until Nick meets him. His true purpose remains shrouded until he needs Nick's help. If the story was told in Gatsby's point of view, it would be impossible to shroud him in mystery. Yes, Nick's point of view serves to increase tension and heighten reveals by exposing information to the reader only when it is timely to do so.

Any time you're wondering if your protagonist has earned enough points to be the point of view character, work through exercise fifteen.

EXERCISE 15: AND THE WINNER IS...

In this exercise, you will assess any point of view character you are working with—regardless of person, tense, number, and distance—using the criteria outlined above.

1. In your journal, write down your point of view character's name and the specifics of the point of view, close, third, first, authorial-omniscient, etc.

2. Answer these questions:
   - Is the perspective she brings to the story unique and interesting?
   - Does she have the most to gain or lose from the story?

- Does her point of view clutter, confuse, or distract from the story in any way?
- Does she ever reduce the tension or spoil reveals?

3. Analyze your answers. Is this point of view earned? If it is, wonderful. If it is not, or is only partly earned, you can cut the point of view or further develop it so that this character does deserve to carry the mantle of point of view.

IF I CAN'T ADD A POINT OF VIEW CHARACTER, NOW WHAT?

Suppose you've begun plotting a story with a single, earned, limited point of view. But then you hit a snag. You believe the reader will be lost if he does not understand some particular machination or other. Some piece of information that is absolutely critical to understanding what is about to happen to your protagonist, even though the protagonist remains in the dark.

And therein lies the problem. Your point of view character cannot reveal the plot point to the reader, and your narrator is not omniscient. How will you show the reader this particular machination if your earned and established point of view character can't know about it herself?

You may be tempted to whip up another point of view character, one in a position to show the reader this critical plot point. You might even think, *I'll only give this guy a few chapters. Short chapters. It won't matter.*

But wait, don't hand over the crown just yet.

Take a deep breath and know you are not the first person to write herself into a corner. It is possible to tell a story, even a series-long story, with a single point of view character. How do you live your life? With a single point of view. Yours. Good and bad things happen to you. You do not have a crystal ball showing you how your life will turn out tomorrow (or maybe you do). Your protagonist definitely does not have a crystal ball. And neither should your reader.

You have options that do not require extra, unearned point of view characters. These options involve the narrator, your best friend. Your narrative exposition offers you ways to introduce story elements that will help the reader track your story. Let's see what they are.

- If your narrator is an authorial-omniscient narrator, life is grand. Working that narrative mojo will allow you to reveal information to the reader.

- If your narrator is limited to the knowledge available to the point of view character, then you need to set up the action with information that is available to the point of view character, without spoiling any reveals. Remember that your narrator has a greater vantage point than your character without being omniscient.

- If your narrator is a first person point of view, he is not the character on the page; he is the older and wiser version of that character. He can reveal things to the reader through narrative exposition that he did not know as the actor in the moment.

- The only narrator who can't help you out of the corner is a first person, present tense narrator. In that case, he simply cannot show the reader anything the protagonist does not already know. If you believe the reader must know something about that plot point that's coming to a head, your protagonist will have to know about it, too. Unfold the complexity of that plot point for the protagonist and the reader by providing enough information to raise intrigue, forming specific questions in the reader's mind that beg to be answered, but not enough to spoil the trouble when the plot point comes fully into play.

- With a third person point of view, your narrator can provide your reader with clues that the point of view character is unaware of. Think of your narrator as watching over your character, but with an eagle's view of the scene. The narrator, like a movie director, can focus the reader's attention on any aspect of the scene. Suppose I describe my character writing a letter, intently concentrating on the paper before her. That description will limit what the reader sees through the point of view character's perspective. My narrator, however, can expand the description, like a camera panning left, to describe the room the character is in. I can come around to the window, and there describe the cars coming up the drive. The narrator has shown the reader the character's world, the character's actions, *and* things the character is unaware of, but that are within the realm of available knowledge.

- You can, in any point of view, provide your point of view character and reader clues that foreshadow what is to come. Then, after the action in question plays out, show the protagonist piecing together how it all came about.

EXERCISE 16: USE YOUR LENS

In this exercise, you will practice controlling your narrative lens. You'll become skillful at showing the reader aspects of your story without relying on your point of view character's perspective. Working with your narrative abilities will help you avoid the temptation to bring an unearned point of view character into the story.

1. Think of a person doing something that requires concentration. It may be a man sitting in a recliner with a book, or a teenager working on needlepoint, or a carpenter at her workbench. Anything will do, so long as you are comfortable describing it.

   – You will begin with an "establishing shot," describing the scene as a whole from the vantage point of being outside and above it.

   – Bring your narrative lens into the scene and show us the character. Describe him physically as you introduce him into the scene.

   – Come in close to the action and show us what he is doing. If he is reading, show us the book. If he is sewing, show us the way he handles his needle and thread and what he is working on.

   – Pull back from the action and show the reader some specific and significant part of the room or environment he is in. Make some aspect of this description emotional. Perhaps a photo of a loved one on a mantel. The description itself should imply the significance of the prop; do not tell, do not resort to dialogue.

- Create a revelation. You might show the reader something in the setting that reveals surprising information about the character, like a wardrobe full of Vaudeville costumes. You might show some sort of intrusion, like the face in the window. You are only limited by the parameters of the scene you are creating.

2. After you've finished the scene, journal about it.
   - What did you learn about the narrative lens?
   - How can you use this to reveal information to the reader or create suspense?
   - Has this exercise further developed your narrative voice? How so?
   - What is the source of tension in your scene?
   - What is interesting about creating a quiet scene with a single character and no dialogue?

RECAP

In this chapter, we looked at what it means to have an earned point of view and how to use your narrator more effectively when you find yourself tempted to create a new point of view character for the sake of revealing information to the reader.

- If you give a character a point of view, it must be earned.

- Each perspective must bear on the story in a unique and interesting way.
- Each point of view character must have something significant to lose or gain.
- The perspective must not clutter, confuse, or distract from the story.
- The perspective must never reduce tension or spoil reveals.
- Exercise 15: And the Winner Is.... In this exercise, you assessed your point of view character using the criteria provided above.
- When the reader must know something the point of view character cannot know, you have several options to work the information into the story.
- Rely more on your narrator and less on your character's perspective to convey the story to your readers.
- Exercise 16: Use Your Lens. In this exercise, you practiced control of your narrative lens by creating a scene with purpose and tension in which the protagonist does not move or speak.

Chapter 14

Don't Dump on Your Reader, or Your Reader Will Dump You

A BIG NARRATIVE NO-NO

Now that I've told you how to bulk up your narrator and give him room to strut his stuff, there are times to rein him in. One such time is the Dread Info Dump.

An *info dump* is when the narrator tries to explain something to the reader and does so in a block of text. Often it is exposition about a setting, a technology, or a concept that has to be explained for the reader to progress in the story. An info dump can also take the shape of a character telling us too much information, information we can glean in subtle and more meaningful ways.

FIXING THE DUMP

You can avoid info dumps by spreading out that information in a scene. The rule for when to present information is simple: present information to the reader when it is relevant to the action on the page. If the information slows the action, cut it, move it, or find a new way to convey it to the reader. Let's look at two info dumps and how the author fixed them.

Here is an excerpt from an early draft of Aldus Baker's *Hidden Ability*. In this passage, we have a classic info dump, common in historical fiction when the writer is "showing his research."

Jalan had seen many sabers. Those favored by the House Yen Lancers were modified backswords. Instead of only one sharp edge, the top edge was also sharp from the tip to about one-third of the way back toward the grip. The blade curved slightly as it approached the tip. There was no sharpened edge at all for several inches right in front of the crossguard. One side of the crossguard swept back and attached to the pommel in order to create a knuckle guard. A centered groove his father had called a fuller ran most of the length along each side of the blade from the crossguard toward the tip. There was something about the craftsmanship of the well-made sabers of House Yen that pleased Jalan. It was all about the look of them because the only one he had ever lifted, his father's, was far too heavy for him to wield. Even when he held the weapon with one hand on the grip and his off hand gripping the blade just in front of the crossguard, it was clear he did not possess the size and strength required.

In the rewrite of this passage, Baker is no longer showing his research, but works the interesting and vivid details of the period into his character's experience, adding both visual and thematic elements to the scene.

Jalan had seen many sabers. He thought of them as elegant weapons. Elegant being a word his mother used to describe gowns, furnishings and various other crafted creations that especially pleased her. The craftsmanship of the well-made sabers of House Yen pleased Jalan. It was the look of them, the slight curve of the blade, the double-edged tip. The only one he had ever lifted, his father's, was far too heavy for him to wield. Even when he held the weapon with one hand on the grip and his off hand gripping the blunt portion of the blade just in front of the crossguard, it felt awkward. He had to lean back in order to keep from tipping forward. Jalan could never hold the weapon with one hand the way the lancers did.

Here is another info dump and its revision. In this scene, men are building a combat training hall.

Jalan watched as men mixed clay, limestone dust, dirt, sand, straw, flax fiber and even some horse dung together. They told Jalan that the mixture would be spread over the lattice of woven sticks to finish each wall panel. It was hard to imagine the men's churned up glop could ever be part of a wall, but as Jalan observed the men fit the lattices and apply the daub, the name they used for their glop, Jalan realized that many of the buildings he saw everyday had walls made in this fashion.

After reading that passage, you might feel it has no place in the story. Does the reader, concerned with Jalen developing his combat skills, care about how walls were made in the medieval period? Probably not, so it would be safe to cut it. Part of what makes historical fiction and fantasy enjoyable for readers, however, is the opportunity to observe life in a distant era. By working those facts into the narrative in a more engaging way, the info dump is transformed into an integral part of the scene, becoming part of Jalen's world and the backdrop to his training session. Here is the revision.

The large rectangular Training Hall had taken shape with the framework of the walls. A series of wooden trusses with interlocking posts supported the roof. Waddle and daub panels filled some of the gaps in the walls. Workmen busied themselves completing more. From inside the building, the wooden skeleton was exposed. No interior wall paneling had yet been placed. Looking up showed an open ceiling all the way through the trusses to the bottom of the roof planks. Six men could easily have stood side-by-side across the width of the hall and—with their arms outstretched—not touch each other or the walls. The length must have been ten men at least. From the floor to the bottom of the roof trusses was nearly the height of two men. Jalan could not understand why the room needed to be so tall. When he mentioned it to Master Enmar, his teacher, gave him another one of his knowing smiles and leapt up to touch a roof truss. Jalan thought he had imagined it. Surely no one could jump that high. Master Enmar simply turned to him and said, "That's why."

In the early draft, Jalen's eyes are a means to an end: show us medieval walls. But in the revision, we again see the building through Jalen's eyes, but this time with a specific question in mind: Why is it so big? When Master Enmar answers his question with a display that can only be called superhuman, we understand why the hall is so big and, more importantly, Baker sets up intrigue: Will Jalen learn to jump like that?

Find out about Aldus Baker at the back of this book.

ACCORDING TO CHEKOV

Suppose your protagonist needs to use a gun, and when the hero picks up said gun to defend herself from the bad guy, the reader learns all about the gun—and the bullets, too!

If your protagonist is fighting for her life, it is not the time to go into great detail about the props she's using. Doing so will slow the pacing, lower the tension, and effectively ruin a climactic scene.

Anton Chekov famously said, "If you introduce a gun in act one, it must go off in act three." In *Dark Corners in Skoghall,* I introduce the gun in act two, but regardless, once it is on the stage of the page, it must be fired. Why an absolute in this world of non-absolutes? Because it's not nice to tease your readers. If you take the time to introduce something into your world and your readers' minds, you must follow through. If you don't, readers who remember the gun will decide you left a loose end, and the Gods of Story will put that in your Log of Craft Errors.

For our purposes, let's invert the Chekov quote: if you are going to fire a gun in act three, you must introduce it in act one or two. The reason to introduce the gun (or whatever prop is relevant to your story) early is so you do not slow down an action scene later.

My protagonist, Jess, has to use a gun in the climax. It is the best reasonable response to the threat she faces. Now, Jess is a peace-loving vegetarian who's never touched a gun in her life. I had to get a gun in her hands and show her how to use it early, so firing the gun on another human being in the climax would be believable. The time to describe the gun is not the climax, it's *never* the climax.

Jess goes to a gun shop and takes a lesson on the firing range. This is clearly not a high-stakes, high-tension scene, but it sets us up for the big one in act three. During the climax, I do not have to describe the gun or tell the reader how many bullets the magazine holds, because I already covered that ground when she bought the gun. This ensures that during the climax, I, Jess, and the reader will all be focused on the threat to Jess and the fact that she has to fire the gun. Without the setup in act two, I would risk readers crying foul, because they wouldn't believe my peace-loving vegetarian, with no prior knowledge of weapons, would point a gun at another human being. And they would be right.

> Set up your action before your action. Do not try to explain things during your action scene.

LEARNING TO SHOOT

Let's check out that scene in *Dark Corners in Skoghall*, discussed above.

Just as Jess stepped into the range, a cannon boomed beside her and she jumped, her hands flailing helplessly near her heart. Fern appeared unaffected as she proceeded past the man with the semiautomatic machine gun to the far end of the range....

"This is a Glock 19," Fern said. She demonstrated to Jess that the magazine was unloaded and the chamber empty, then put it in Jess's hands.

It weighed less than Jess had expected, looked surprisingly uncomplicated, and scared her, but she wasn't going to admit that to Lumberjack Fern.

"Now," Fern continued, "let's teach you how to use this thing." She took the gun from Jess and demonstrated how to handle it, naming all its parts while discussing gun safety. "The first rule is to always treat it like it's loaded and only point it in a safe direction." She showed Jess how to load the magazine. "These are nine mil Parabellum bullets," she said. "The mag will hold fifteen bullets, which means the gun can take sixteen. The mag plus one in the chamber." She slid bullets into the magazine like she was loading candy into a PEZ dispenser. When she'd inserted five bullets, she handed it to Jess.

Getting the bullets in the magazine took some getting used to. She had to press down while angling the bullet just right. Sometimes the lip of the bullet she was loading stuck on the line where the brass case met the copper head of the bullet beneath it. When the "cannon" at the other end of the range boomed, Jess's fingers slipped and she dropped a bullet. She stared at it lying between the toes of Fern's work boots. Fern bent and swept it up. "Don't worry," she said, handing the bullet back to Jess. "It takes a lot more than that to make one of these go off."

Fern showed Jess how to slide the magazine into the grip. "The bullets always point uphill. If they point downhill, you'll jam the gun. That's bad." *That's bad* seemed like an understatement to Jess. She didn't want to find out what would happen if she inserted a bullet backwards in the chamber. Fern removed the magazine and continued the lesson with the gun unloaded. "This is the slide. It'll tear your knuckle off if you don't hold the gun properly." Fern put the gun in Jess's hands and made sure she had her thumbs down. Then Fern looked at Jess's feet. "That's an isosceles stance," she tapped Jess's feet with one of her own while using her hands to rotate Jess's elbows. "You want to absorb the recoil into your chest, instead of up into your face."

"That's a lot to keep straight."

"It's easier than you think. Remember driver's ed? Remember being told about gears and mirrors and signals and pedals? And then it all became so easy you could drive without hardly paying attention to the car?" Fern handed Jess the magazine. "Load your gun."

Jess looked at the top bullet, inspecting its angle and making certain it pointed uphill before sliding it into the Glock's grip. She looked at Fern, uncertain what came next. Again the machine gun shook the range.

Fern grabbed the Glock's slide and pulled it back, exposing the barrel, then released it so it snapped forward. "Now the gun is loaded and this is a live weapon." Fern laid it on the counter in front of them, barrel pointing down range, and stepped back.

Jess picked up the gun, took her stance, rotated her elbows, all the things Fern had taught her, and looked down the barrel at her target. "Curve your back slightly forward, like you're going off a diving board," Fern said, her voice surprisingly easy to hear through the ear muffs. "Dot the i in your sights." Jess stared, trying not to squint one eye shut, and lined up the sights with the bulls-eye. She squeezed the trigger with the pad of her finger, as instructed, taking up the slack, then felt the resistance when the trigger engaged. It took forever to pull the trigger, holding her breath, her concentration so focused that she registered the sound of the machine gun being fired nearby without startling. She drew the trigger the rest of the way and the gun fired with a loud crack and jerked upwards in Jess's hands. She glimpsed the muzzle flash as the brass case ejected, arcing up and back past her head.

The scene is detailed, and I chose to include the specifics about the weapon while Jess receives her lesson. In order to ensure the scene will interest my reader—including those who do not care about gun specs—I focused on Jess's experience of firing the gun, instead of on the gun itself. I presented the information in a scene with a new, secondary supporting character—one I like and intend to bring back in future books. Fern provides the technical specs about the weapon in dialogue. The setting, the man firing a machine gun next to Jess, and the action of Jess handling the gun all contribute to making this a full scene, and not an info dump. Importantly, Jess provides the emotional context for the scene. Keep in mind, the emotional context goes beyond the scene itself. Fear for her life has compelled her to visit the shooting range.

DON'T BE FOOLED

Sometimes a character delivers an info dump in dialogue. Just because "he said" is tacked onto the end of a block of text does not mean the writer has escaped the Dread Info Dump. If that monologue reads like an info dump, it is one. Treat it the same as you would a narrative dump.

EXERCISE 17: AVOIDING THE DREAD INFO DUMP

In this exercise, you'll explore ways to avoid info dumps.

1. You'll begin by freewriting a scene in which you explain to your reader how a machine works. You can use whatever point of view you like for this scene, but use narrative exposition to explain how the machine works.
   - Your machine could be a table saw, a tractor, a sewing machine, a car. Choose one you can explain easily.
   - Describe it. Then explain to the reader what the machine is for and how it works.
   - Set a timer for fifteen minutes. Ready? Go!
2. Read your scene. You should have a nice block of text, an info dump, explaining the machine to your reader.
3. Rewrite the scene. This time, have two characters approach the machine. Use dialogue to convey the information in that block of text in the first scene. Have your two characters

discuss the machine in such a way that the reader learns how it works.

Try to make the dialogue natural. It should not be a reprint of the info dump broken into lines with dialogue tags. Set a timer for fifteen minutes. Ready? Go!

4. Rewrite the scene again. This time, convey the information as brief lines of exposition woven through an action scene. Have your two characters work the machine and move around to make the machine function. Feed the reader the necessary information when it is most appropriate to the action and most engaging for the reader. You can use dialogue here, too, as fitting, since you have two characters working together.

Set a timer for fifteen minutes. Ready? Go!

5. Compare your three scenes. Answer these questions in your journal:

   – Which scene was the easiest to write? The hardest? Why?

   – Which scene is the most enjoyable to read? Why?

   – Were you able to convey emotion in your scene? How? How does it change the impact of the scene?

   – What have you learned about conveying necessary information to readers that you can now apply to your writing of narrative exposition?

RECAP

In this chapter, we explored the Dread Info Dump and how to avoid it. Info dumps are blocks of narrative exposition that slow down action. They are also a poor use of your narrator.

- Info dumps are passages of narrative that exist solely to feed the reader information. That information may be necessary, but it must not read like it exists solely for the reader's sake.
- Present information when it is relevant.
- If the information slows a scene's action, cut it, move it, or find another way to present it.
- Set up your action before the action scene.
- Use dialogue, action, and brief sections of exposition to present information that is necessary to the story, emotionally relevant to your point of view character, and intriguing to the reader.
- Adding "she said" to the end of an info dump does not make it other than an info dump.
- Exercise 17: Avoiding the Dread Info Dump. In this exercise, you wrote an info dump, then found ways to reshape the information, so it did not slow your action, while controlling your narrative voice and exposition.

Chapter 15

Effectively Affecting Your Reader

WRITERS ARE MEAN

As writers, we get to be...well, cruel to our readers. We manipulate their emotions to suit our whims. Go ahead and delight in that for a moment. We aren't bad people. We are artists and making people *feel* is in the job description. In fact, it is why people read stories—to feel things they can't or won't get to experience in their own lives.

Perhaps *whims* is the wrong word, because in reality we must carefully craft our narratives with an intended effect in mind. And that effect is the one that will best reveal the story to the reader in the most appropriately charged way. We need to craft our narrative journeys so the whole is composed of hundreds of moments, each different from but building upon the last until, together, we reach the story's climax.

> The skilled craftsperson manipulates
> every detail of her material
> with a final design in mind.

After all, could you call yourself a horror writer if you did not try to scare your readers? Or a romance writer if you did not intend to tug at your readers' heartstrings? Or a mystery writer if you did not present a red herring or two to confuse your sleuthing readers?

MASTER MANIPULATORS

You will use all of the tools in your writer's toolbox to craft a story that will have your intended effect on the reader. Primary among those tools are your narrative and point of view character's perspective. Everything you've learned about point of view has been preparing you to consciously choose how you want to manipulate your readers' emotions.

Describe the reaction you expect your reader to have to a given scene in your story, and you've just identified the intended effect of that scene. Your intended effect will vary from scene to scene, depending on its content and how it advances the story. You may even have more than one intended effect in a given scene. Your setting might create a certain mood, while your character evokes pity. I mentioned *Ethan Frome* in chapter four, "Heart Your Narrator." The mood I experienced, which is one effect we can assume Wharton intended to achieve, is that I felt the cold, bleak winter setting coming alive, despite my world being its opposite. I also experienced pity and grief for the title character, Ethan, because he fell in love with a woman he could never have, then suffered her tragic death. Wharton made Ethan a sympathetic character, so we can assume pity and grief are among her intended effects upon the reader.

During the climax of *Dark Corners in Skoghall,* my intention is for the reader to feel tense, worried for the hero, anxious about the bad guy possibly escaping, and thrilled by the drama. That may seem like a lot, but any climax in a crime-related story should aim for a similar effect.

If you're writing a touching scene, your goal should be for the reader to feel . . . touched. Maybe the scene is bittersweet, maybe it's beautiful, maybe it's tragic, but during the scene, if you're writing effectively, the reader will be moved.

Keep in mind, a climax is relative to its story. In a romantic comedy, the intended effect of the climax is going to be something like romantic elation, a happy, warm-fuzzy feeling in the chest of the reader. And nobody has to fire a gun to achieve that effect.

In *The Story Works Guide to Writing Character,* I wrote a scene in which Mark goes home for his father's funeral. There's a flashback to when his father ran him off with a shotgun. If I have written it well, every reader will feel some effect from this scene. One reader might become angry, another sad, and another might sympathize with the father. We cannot control the specifics of a reader's reaction, but if we make him feel something along with the character, we are doing our job well.

Here is the Mark scene again. See what effect it has on you and how that effect has been achieved.

Snow covered the fields lining the road, and the sun wouldn't be up for over an hour yet. The Ford Focus, an economy rental, was comfortable in an economy sort of way. Mark couldn't get his phone's Bluetooth and the car's stereo to connect, so he'd been driving with just the noise of his tires on the road for company since he left the metro over an hour ago. The coffee he bought at the airport was giving him a stomachache. A garment bag hung in the back seat with a black suit in it. He didn't know if he'd put the suit on. It could be overkill out here in the sticks. Or it could be expected by the farming crowd, always more traditional and more conservative than he could stand. The rotgut caused by the airport coffee only got worse the closer he got to his boyhood home. A home he had not seen since the day his old man had run him off with a shotgun in hand.

Mark lifted the screen door as he opened it so the hinges wouldn't squeak. "Early to bed, early to rise" had long been his parents' motto, which made missing curfew an easy temptation to satisfy—so long as he didn't get caught sneaking in. He stepped over the threshold into the house, turned around and carefully shut the door behind him. They never locked anything, living way out in the boonies like they did. It took twenty minutes on the best day just to get into town. That seemed justification enough for staying out late, gallivanting around, as his mother liked to say. Mark put a hand against the wall to steady himself and reached down with his other hand to unlace his sneakers. His mother had a shoes-at-the-door policy that didn't apply to his parents. He'd stopped questioning such inconsistencies long ago.

Mark turned away from the door and crept toward the staircase. He put a hand on the banister, a foot on the first step. A light snapped on in the living room.

Mark's father sat in the green recliner—he'd turned it around to face the entryway—with his shotgun across his lap. His cleaning kit sat open on the side table, under the lamp he'd just turned on. Mark's heart caught somewhere high in his chest. The cleaning kit seemed like a prop, a ruse, to avert suspicion for an act that had yet to be committed.

"'Night, Dad." He turned to face the stairs, lifted his foot to bring it to the next step.

"Is it true?"

"Is what true?" His voice sounded small. It was the voice of an intruder.

"I heard the things some of the boys said about you, but I did not want to believe them. And then Dale..." Dale was a mean old gossip. If someone's troubles weren't big enough, Dale could be counted on to exaggerate them into fact. "He said he seen you coming out of a deer blind with that Johnsen kid."

"We...we were just having a beer, Dad. Shooting the shit and getting messed up. Like you and Dale do every Saturday." Mark clenched the handrail and looked up, hoping to find a saving grace at the top of the stairs.

"Thing is, Dale had his binoculars on him. He saw you. He saw what you did with that Johnsen kid."

This was possible. The blind they'd chosen consisted of a frame draped with camouflage netting. It belonged to Mark's cousin, and he was at work. It was also, they had thought, set away from the most-used trails. Leave it to Dale to come trudging through their part of the woods and to not leave well enough alone.

His father rose from the chair and came toward Mark, the shotgun in his hands. The natural thing would have been to set it down, lean it against the chair or the wall, but he hung onto it, held it across his chest like he'd been taught in the army. Ready, aim, fire came all too easily to this man. Mark rocked on his feet, uncertain which way to go. Should he launch himself up the stairs, deeper into his father's house? Or hurl himself backwards, at the door and the world outside?

It had turned out it wasn't Mark's decision to make; his father had a plan.

Mark slammed on the brakes. The rental stopped quicker than he'd expected and Mark lurched forward, his seatbelt locking across his chest, then pinning him to his seat. He fumbled with the latch, released the belt buckle, and finally threw open the door. Mark tumbled out of the car onto the gravel road and vomited what remained of the coffee and a breakfast burrito.

How did that scene affect you? Why?

Each reader may experience a different shade of the intended effect, but they should all be similar enough that the writer can assess whether or not the scene has accomplished her goal. In this scene, I want the reader to share Mark's anxiety about going home by understanding the source of it and sympathizing with him. I want the scene to create tension through the expectation that Mark's homecoming will be uncomfortable, if not unpleasant.

At some point in your writing, you should be able to articulate what effect you want a scene to have on a reader. To do that, consider what your scene is about, the thematic content of your scene. The scene above is about family and the things that tear them apart, in this case homophobia. It could have been about any number of issues that might cause a parent to reject a child. But the scene is only partly about parents rejecting children. The point of view character, Mark, is an adult, making a free choice to come home for his father's funeral, so the scene is about going home, facing your past, growing into yourself, and recognizing your parents' limitations. Any one of those thematic elements could resonate with a reader, and each reader could identify and be affected by a different aspect of the scene. All of the readers would be correct. My intention is not to limit what aspect of the story readers resonate with, but to ensure they have an emotional experience of the scene. In this case, we might describe the intended effect as "anxious anticipation of an uncomfortable homecoming."

Set your intended effect when you write and expect a range of interpretations when your story reaches readers.

EXERCISE 18: EFFECTIVE EFFECTS

In this exercise, you will assess a number of scenes for the effect on the reader and how they are achieved. Grab a bunch of books. Read a scene or two from each book with your journal on hand. Choose scenes from random places in the books—don't read all opening scenes or all climactic scenes. Answer the following questions for each scene. For an example, I will answer the questions for the Mark scene.

1. What is the scene about in plot terms and in thematic terms?
    -   Plot: Going home for the father's funeral.
    -   Theme: Parent-child estrangement, homophobia, facing your past.

2. What effect does the scene have on you as a reader? If the scene seems ineffective, note that and address why.
    -   I, as reader, empathize with Mark's anxiety about going home and facing an uncertain reception.

3. How does the author achieve that effect?
    -   I, as author, show Mark's physical discomfort growing as he gets closer to the farm—upset stomach, bad memories, vomiting.
    -   I use flashback to show us when he left home and how awful that was, his father holding a gun while telling him to get out.
    -   I leave questions unanswered to build intrigue. Where is the mother? Does Mark have any money or clothing when he leaves, or does his dad toss him out with only what's on his back?

4. How is point of view used to create or enhance the desired effect?

- This scene is a close, third person point of view. The reader is in the car with Mark, aware of his anxiety, and enters his thoughts to go into the flashback.

- The flashback has more emotional distance—that part of the scene is in the distant past. It shows a turning point in Mark's life. The flashback also shows the reader the baggage Mark is toting around and how the past is triggering his anxiety. But the focus of the scene is the now. As the result of narrative distance, the reader, while feeling for the teenager who gets kicked out, should be feeling more for the adult who is about to face his past.

> Action in the present trumps
> action in the past.

MORE ABOUT READER EMPATHY

I always say that character is the heart of your story and we humans are hardwired for empathy. And empathy is the reason readers identify with the main character and are willing to follow him for three hundred pages. The point of view character is the one we get to know intimately by being inside his head and feelings, by understanding his worldview and personal stakes in life. How do you get your reader to empathize with your point of view character?

We can illustrate this simply.

Suppose you are reading the newspaper and see an article about a house burning down. How emotional do you feel hearing that a stranger somewhere lost a home?

Now suppose you're on the phone with your mother and she tells you that your cousin in North Dakota lost his home to a fire last week. How much emotion do you feel for that out-of-town cousin's lost home?

Now suppose sirens wake you in the middle of the night. Your neighbor's house is on fire. You stand beside your neighbor, who is also a dear friend, with your arm around her shoulder. How much emotion do you feel comforting your friend as her home is destroyed?

There are three factors at play in the examples above. To write scenes that create your desired effects, you need to employ all of them.

Connection: You will feel more for your cousin, even a cousin you don't know very well, than a stranger. Spending time with someone, getting to know her, and understanding her world all contribute to a sense of connection. You'll probably feel more connected to your friend and neighbor than a cousin who lives in a different state, because you see her frequently and know her better than that cousin.

You know the spectacle of trauma and you know about personal loss, or you will one day. When you write trauma into your story without giving the reader time to bond with your point of view character, you create *spectacle*. That can be very effective, so long as spectacle is your goal. When you write trauma into your story after the reader has developed a connection with your point of view character, you create *tragedy*. If your character's house burns down in the opening scene of your book, the focus will be on the spectacle of the fire and the general understanding we all have of loss. It will function as a hook, not a climax. Later in your story, when the reader knows your character and feels connection, the effect on the reader will be personal, because the reader will be more engaged with your character.

Immediacy: Experiencing the fire as it happens will have a greater impact on you than the news from your mother or a newspaper because of the immediacy and "realness" of the moment. An experience always trumps a report. In the face of immediate danger, even if it is not our own, we have the urge to get up and do something about it. Events shown in-scene, in the *now*-story, always beat events learned about through dialogue, summary, or exposition.

Sensory Details: Using sensory details is critical to creating a sense of immediacy and connection. You and your reader will feel most strongly for the neighbor, because you experience the fire. This is another example of "show, don't tell." You see the flames consume the house, smell the smoke, and feel the heat. You watch with your friend as the firefighters do their job. If she cries, you might cry with her. You try to console her, but end up feeling helpless.

The same is true for your reader and point of view character. The goal is to write the experience your character lives in such a way that the reader feels he is there, living it with your character. Those sensory details make the experience real for the reader and will enhance the empathy your reader feels for the point of view character.

In fiction, writers must employ all three narrative factors to create a scene that evokes the strongest emotions in readers.

Note: If you want to write a powerful scene to show something from your character's backstory, then you'll need to use flashback, not narrative exposition or dialogue, as I did in the Mark scene above. I covered writing backstory and flashbacks in detail in *The Story Works Guide to Writing Character*.

> To effectively affect your reader, put your point of view character in the middle of action happening in the now-story full of sensory details.

PLAINS AND PEAKS

Your narrative voice is a powerful tool when used effectively to show, not tell. Showing creates emotional currency. You want your narrative to be as much of a lived experience as you can create. In the world of story, with plot arcs and character arcs, the narrative should never be flat.

> When you tell, you create an emotional plain. When you show, you create an emotional peak.

This is an emotional plain.

I felt bad, because my family was losing the house and my siblings and I would be starting over again.

This is a peak.

I ran home from school, the whole stretch of five city blocks, leaping across intersections without a thought for the afternoon traffic, because I was invincible. I held the crumpled paper in my sweaty fist. The top of the page rippled like a flag, and every few strides I glanced at it to make sure it was still there. Still real. The capital A, circled, in red felt-tip pen. The first one I had ever seen atop a paper with my name on it, the first one my mother would ever see next to one of her children's names, a triumph.

There were people standing on the front porch of the little bungalow with peeling blue paint and a leaking roof. Three large men. I slowed, and my joy drained out of me. I walked up the sidewalk, panting from my run, my brow creased as I assessed today's trouble. When I got closer, I saw my mother and little brother and sister standing outside. My mother had an arm around each of my siblings and she looked at the men, her face an expression of pleading. I barreled forward, my A forgotten, dropped in front of the neighbor's house, and where it blew to I have no idea. I charged up the porch steps and pushed through the big men. I wanted to wrap my arms around my mother's legs and cling to her the way my sister did, her thumb in her mouth and her rag of a blanket draped over one shoulder. But what kind of show would that make for these men? I spun and faced them, planted my hands on my hips, and glared at them.

One of the men, I saw now, was Mr. Hurley, our landlord. His lips twitched at the corners, but he refrained from smiling. He took off his hat and held it before him in a show of gentlemanly conduct, but he could not fool me. There was nothing gentlemanly about this visit. "Hello, Daniel," he said.

"What's going on here?" I demanded.

"Daniel." My mother's voice was soft, crackling the way voices do when a person has been crying but trying not to.

I looked at Mr. Hurley as fiercely as I could.

"Well," he cleared his throat. "Your mother has been locked out."

"You can't do that!" I shouted, sounding much more like a kid than I'd intended.

"Do you have three months' rent on you, young man?"

I dropped my gaze to my shoes, to the hole where the canvas had worn away, separating from the rubber toe. *Dang it,* I thought. I looked over my shoulder at my mother, then down at her feet, at her scuffed brown shoes with the heel that had to be glued back in place every few weeks. That was when I noticed the suitcases behind her, just two of them, as weary as we were.

EXERCISE 19: CLIMBING THE PEAK

In this exercise, you'll study the scene above to further develop your understanding of narrative elements and how they come together to create an emotional experience for the reader.

- Go through the scene about Daniel's family getting locked out and answer the following questions in your journal.
  - List everything Daniel feels over the course of this scene.
  - List everything you feel with or for Daniel and his family as you read the scene.
  - How many emotional shifts occur? For Daniel? For you?
  - How do the words evoke these emotions? Look at the use of action, dialogue, and narrative. Notice how those three aspects of story are woven together in this brief scene.
  - What elements in this scene create a feeling of connection to the characters?
  - What elements create a sense of immediacy?
  - How are sensory details used in this scene?
  - What do you discover about the people in this scene? Make a list. Consider the setting, possible time and place for this scene, economics, age, power dynamics, relationships and how the characters feel about each other, and anything else that comes to mind.
  - How do you discover all of those things?
  - What have you learned by examining this scene that you can now apply to your own writing?

RECAP

In this chapter, we examined the primary goal of any writer: to make the reader feel something. We discussed some key narrative elements to help you identify the goal for each scene and then execute it effectively.

- Part of your job as a writer is to manipulate your reader's emotions.

- Set your intended effect for each scene you write and craft it to accomplish that emotional goal.

- Exercise 18: Effective Effects. In this exercise, you looked at a variety of scenes to assess their effect on the reader and if they were effective in accomplishing the author's assumed goal.

- Understand that you may affect your reader in a variety of ways, including some you do not intend. A reader's experience of your story will be individual to that reader.

- Key to creating an emotional experience on the page is reader empathy, which is greatly enhanced when you use connection, immediacy, and sensory details in your scenes.

- Use your narrative voice to show, not tell. Telling creates emotional plains. Showing creates emotional peaks.

- Exercise 19: Climbing the Peak. In this exercise, you examined a scene to develop your understanding of narrative elements and how they come together to create an emotional experience for the reader.

Special Section

Name That Point of View!

Now that you know all about point of view, let's work with some examples. I've collected a handful of excerpts here. After you read each one, make some notes in your journal, identifying the point of view and how it affected your experience of the story. Then read the notes that follow each excerpt.

The basic elements of point of view are:

- Person: first, second, third;
- Tense: past, present;
- Number: single, multiple, omniscient; and
- Distance: close, middle, distant.

Understanding and controlling
point of view gives you the power
to craft a specific, desirable
experience of your story.

LEELAND ARTRA'S
IMPOSSIBLE PARADISE

This is the opening of the book, so no set up is required.

Squee...click...rrmm...thunk-thunk-thunk

It's working now, sir.

"I just sit here and talk into that thing?"

Yes, sir. Do you need help?

"Lady, I know I look as old as dirt. But, I'm not a cobbly sailor yet. I can manage."

Of course, sir.

Thunk-Thunk.

"So this thing will let people hear what we're saying right now, in the future?"

Yes sir, our voices will be preserved for visitors to listen to, like reading a book. As I explained when we first met, the Empress desires an accurate record of the events leading up to this age by those who were directly involved. It's my greatest honor to interview you as part of this initiative. This will be a priceless treasure for future generations. We're under strict orders to censor nothing. I'm only here to serve you, sir.

"Hmm."

Sir. Are you okay? Do you need a handkerchief?

"Yes, yes. I'd thought I'd seen it all. But, this thing is... well...amazing. Lady Janali, Empresses bless her, would have loved to see it. I'm not so sure I can do this."

I understand, sir. Perhaps it would be better if you ignore that and speak to me. I want to hear your story as you remember it.

"Well, ma'am, that's a course I can navigate. Get one of them helpers to bring us some hot java, and we'll start."

You can call me Captain Reinvo. What house I was born to don't matter 'cause they didn't bother to keep me past my mother's milk. The merchant marine commune records might show where I came from, but I've never looked.

The facts of the matter are simple enough. On Martidi, Tarudyt twenty-fourth, 14343—that is the third day of the week on the twenty-fourth day of the second month of spring by the old calendar—the Vibrius set out from the imperial capital harbor for his suitor voyage. The first ship of his kind. He had a set of twin screw shafts driven with multi-stroke steam engines instead of the ordinary single stroke steam piston engine connected to a pair of paddle wheels. The propellers made everyone overlook the fact he was also the first ship made of iron.

I accepted command of the Vibrius because he was the most handsome and faithful ship I'd ever set eyes upon. The child of Lady Janali Jedalor's repressed scientific genius. What mattered to House Jedalor, the house I served most of my adult life, was that the Vibrius was big. The iron construction allowed the Vibrius to be built larger than any ship before. The propeller drive, lack of paddle wheels, and extra size gave the Vibrius almost double the cargo space of his closest rival. And that was why House Jedalor allowed Lady Janali to build him.

Lady Janali was House Jedalor's castatan. Except, she always seemed to be sailing into the wind as castatan. Sure, she maneuvered well enough to perform her duty as business leader for House Jedalor. But, I saw her working in the Anev shipyards, her clothes covered in grease and grime, and twin fires in her eyes as she built the Vibrius. She was glorious as she bent metal, machine, and man to her goals. When she spoke, every engineer around stopped to listen.

When I took command, Lady Janali said she'd done the math, and I could push the Vibrius's engines harder than any ship I'd ever commanded. She ordered me to complete the northern trade route in not less than three-quarters the normal trip time and to barter hard, making sure to bring him back full of cargo.

We did just as she wanted. Better even.

Until—exactly four weeks after setting out from the capital—the entire world changed.

Before you read on, take a minute to consider the passage and identify the point of view. Then consider how the point of view shapes the story and its effect on you as a reader. Make notes in your journal. Answer the questions below for yourself before reading my answers.

- **Person:** First.
- **Tense:** Present.
- **Number:** Single.
- **Distance:** Distant.

Why would the author have written this story with this point of view? What are the possible benefits to this style?

This is an interesting excerpt, because Artra shifts the point of view. In the first section, Captain Reinvo is speaking into a microphone, and it's as though we're hearing the recording, and not sitting in the room with him. As a result, Reinvo does not narrate per se. The story opens with a few lines of dialogue. Those lines, nonetheless, serve to introduce the scenario and our narrator as a character. He is telling his story to preserve it in some kind of new technology.

Once he begins telling the tale, he functions as narrator, but it reads like a transcript of the recording, minus coughs or shuffling noises. Although a first person narrator, he is telling a story that focuses on Lady Janali and the Vibrius more so than on his own experiences and emotions, so the psychic connection is distant, not intimate.

This introduction with a storyteller as narrator frames the main story. Once the introduction is made and we have a sense of the opening scenario, Artra switches the point of view again. Here begins the main story.

Captain Reinvo stepped out of the bridge to smell the salty air. He tied his rain hat in place and cinched up his heavy weather jacket against the spraying winds. The skies continued to darken, and the *Vibrius* swayed heavily as the storm's waves grew stronger. He took in a deep breath of the charged air, the hairs on his arms standing up as his skin prickled with energy. His gut tightened. They were heading into a gale.

The iron deck hummed under his feet as the engines poured their energy into the strait's waters. A flock of gray seabirds' screams barely cut over the wind and seas as they sailed in the *Vibrius's* draft. Looking down on the waters, he could see the twin foam trails from the new screw-driven propellers.

Open waters were close. The channel was wide enough but lined with shallow reefs. The winds were down channel, and he considered attempting to turn back to Aedon. They were only a few hours out of port; if they turned about, they could easily make it back to the safe harbor. It would be dangerous for a ship the size of the *Vibrius*, especially with these winds.

Commander Ardlee, his second in command, climbed the deck ladder and saluted. "Sir, all the hatches are tight. Sails are secured." Ardlee's vibrant voice crackled from the volume of his yelling over the noise.

Reinvo looked up at the sky. "This is going to be stronger than we expected," he called back.

He grabbed Ardlee's shoulder and pulled the officer closer. "Engines to a hundred and ten percent. Sound general quarters. I want every man in storm gear and double safety lines 'til we are clear of the reefs," he said into Ardlee's closest ear.

Ardlee's lips tightened. "Sir, we haven't tested the engines above eighty percent."

Reinvo pointed at the cliffs that marked the end of the channel before they'd be clear into the open waters of the northern ocean. Ardlee leaned in close to listen. "We are in the draft of the Othane Plateau. When we come around it, the winds will have us. Empresses know, I'm praying the storm's not as strong as I think. But, I have more faith in Lady Janali's engineering than that prayer. We need to be a bullet out of the muzzle to clear the reefs."

Commander Ardlee saluted and stepped into the bridge to give the orders.

Before you read on, take a minute to consider the passage and identify the point of view. Then consider how the point of view shapes the story and its effect on you as a reader. Make notes in your journal. Answer the questions below for yourself before reading my answers.

- **Person:** Third.
- **Tense:** Past.
- **Number:** Single.
- **Distance:** Close.

Why would the author have written this story with this point of view? What are the possible benefits to this style?

Whether Artra intended for the reader to be in the room with Reinvo when he makes the recording or listening to the recording later, the style of the framing passage is not engaging enough to sustain a novel. That's because Reinvo is a good storyteller, but not a good narrator. In fact, it is useful to look at this excerpt again to see the difference between telling a story *about* one's experiences and narrating a written story.

This frame does work well as a hook and introduction. Reinvo is a likable character and the scenario is established in a quick, engaging manner. Reinvo, however, is an underqualified first person narrator, which left Artra with the choice of either increasing Reinvo's narrative prowess or stripping him of narrative duties.

Either choice would have been fine, but Artra chose the latter. One likely reason is that this book is part of a series. Narrative continuity across a series is a wise choice for any writer.

We know from the very beginning that this is a steampunk adventure story. The noises the recording device makes are our first clue. As Reinvo begins his tale, he talks about steam engines and this ship being the first one ever made of iron. We also learn in the framing passage that the story is one of adventure and danger, which Reinvo survived. This adventure somehow led into a new age. The stakes are high, but the outcome is assured, because whatever we are about to read is leading this world into a new era. If Artra had not used the framing technique with the character-narrator, his authorial narrator would not have been able to tell us this. Why?

His main narrative is in the limited, close third, so the narrator cannot tell us anything the point of view character, Reinvo, can't know. This increases dramatic tension in the opening scene. Reinvo is preparing his men and his ship to enter a mighty storm. At that moment in time, Reinvo does not know he will survive. The reader does, but nothing more.

If Reinvo had narrated the main story from the moment in time when he is speaking into the recording device, he would know more than both himself and the limited narrator in that opening scene. And he may have been tempted to spoil dramatic tension. He might say, "That storm, it was as bad as I had thought, but the engines performed just as I'd hoped and everything turned out fine." Of course, Artra would have been able to maintain dramatic tension with a first person narrator by controlling what the narrator reveals to the reader. In the limited, third person point of view, however, the issue is moot because the narrator can only reveal information available to the point of view character at that time.

Find out about Leeland Artra at the back of this book.

CHRIS FOX'S *NO MERE ZOMBIE*

Before reading this excerpt, you should know that Irakesh is an ancient Egyptian god, the deathless are zombies, and some of the characters, including Cyntia, are werewolves. The excerpts are taken from three separate chapters.

"Observe carefully, Trevor," Irakesh instructed, turning to face the throng of nascent deathless before him. They crowded the inside of the hangar, packing the area between the odd metal conveyances that these moderns referred to as airplanes. "I am going to create an Anakim, one of the most potent servants the deathless possess."

"A giant?" Cyntia rumbled, her blonde fur barely visible in the near darkness.

Irakesh was genuinely surprised. It should have been impossible for any memory of the Anakim to survive. "Just so. How do you know of them?"

"From the Bible," Cyntia explained, giving a furry shrug. "The Anakim were giants. My mother used to scare me with stories when I was little."

"You're going to make a biblical giant?" Trevor asked, raising an eyebrow. He rested the barrel of a rifle against his shoulder, the weapon cradled with the same casual familiarity Irakesh exhibited with his na-kopesh.

"A giant, yes. But I seriously doubt it will resemble anything from your silly book," Irakesh said, turning back to the horde of nascent deathless. He scanned the crowd, looking for the best candidate to begin his work. "There. Do you see that one with the bristly hair? The tall one."

The deathless he'd indicated stood at least seven feet tall, an extreme rarity in Irakesh's time. It was heavily muscled, probably a combatant in one of the games the moderns called sports.

* * *

"What's your plan, Blair?" Steve asked, more than a little smug. He shifted, his clothing vanishing into his midnight fur. How the hell did he do that?

"I can feel him that way," Blair said, pointing towards the farthest of the bulky shapes. It was a massive cargo plane of the kind used in every military movie from the past two decades. Large and squat with four engines and a long ramp extending down the back. "He's inside that plane. Right now. We just have to get there."

"That's going to be a problem," Steve said, grabbing Blair's shoulder. He pointed into the darkness. "A big problem."

The ground shook as a massive figure pounded a path towards them. It towered over the other zombies, a good ten or eleven feet tall and wider than any linebacker he'd ever seen. The thing made Liz-wolf look like a puppy. The giant resembled the other zombies, pale flaccid skin and too-white, razored teeth. Yet where they wore dull vacant expressions its eyes shone green with cunning. Where they shambled it thundered, massive muscles bunching as it surged towards them. It moved so swiftly, knocking shorter zombies aside like kindling as it approached.

"Move," Blair roared, rolling out of the thing's path. It thundered past, leaving the stench of death in its wake. He shot to his feet, turning to Steve. "Get something sharp and stab it in the spine. I'll distract it."

"Got it," Steve shot back, blurring to the door of the Cessna. He yanked it open and disappeared inside.

Blair turned his attention back to the huge deathless just in time to receive a meaty fist to the face. It shattered his jaw, sending bone fragments rattling through his skull. He blanked, coming to in a heap against a wall. There were gaps. Pieces missing. So many things danced out of reach. How badly hurt was he? The ground shook as something large approached. Damn him for a fool. Why hadn't he waited for everyone?

* * *

Liz flung open the jeep's door, kicking off the seat with enough force to send the vehicle skidding across the pavement. She landed in a crouch near the doorway her two companions had just disappeared through. Damn Blair and damn Steve for following him. If he wasn't already dead she was going to kill him. They should have attacked as a group, but those two school kids had rushed blindly ahead.

"Bridget, through the door to the right. I'll go left. Jordan, follow and watch our backs," Liz commanded, low voice rumbling like a semi.

Bridget's silver form leapt through the door, managing majestic if not beautiful. In contrast, Liz probably resembled a very large pit bull whose territory had just been invaded, ungainly but undeniable.

She sprinted through the door, gathering the shadows close about her as she entered the dim. A chorus of familiar low moans echoed through the hangar, obscuring most other noise. The exception was the din of combat coming from somewhere near the center, the area obscured by two bulky planes. She heard the low grunts that were probably Blair and Steve, followed by a hollow boom as something empty was struck with massive force. . . .

The trio flowed with incredible synergy despite having only worked together for a few weeks. Jordan mercilessly cut down the zombies trying to close ranks behind them, while she and Bridget mowed a wide path through the hangar. They rounded one of the planes, this one a mid-sized Cessna like the one Garland had flown. As she rounded the plane's white nose she finally saw Blair, his silver body shattered and broken against the wheel of another plane.

A huge zombie loomed over Blair, taller than her by at least a couple feet. The thing seemed consternated by the plane in the way, leaning back and forth as if unsure how to reach him. Its limbs were too long, chest too broad. The ungainly creature finally dropped to its knees and extended an arm under the plane. It patted the ground a few feet to Blair's left, searching. It wouldn't be long until it found him.

Blam.

A gunshot cracked behind her. Right behind her. She jerked around, expecting to see Jordan killing a zombie. What she found turned her innards to ice and constricted her throat with death's black hands. Jordan lay in a pool of his own blood, both fanged face and furry chest an unrecognizable mess. That she might have been able to process, but it was the attacker that untied her like a pair of shoelaces. It was Trevor.

For one tiny shaving of a moment she caught his gaze, eyes horribly green just like Irakesh. His teeth, too white and razor-sharp. Trevor was her brother, but everything in

STORY WORKS GUIDE TO WRITING POINT OF VIEW

her cried that he needed to be destroyed. Then he vanished, slipping into the shadows just as she would have.

Before you read on, take a minute to consider the passage and identify the point of view. Then consider how the point of view shapes the story and its effect on you as a reader. Make notes in your journal. Answer the questions below for yourself before reading my answers.

- **Person:** Third.
- **Tense:** Past.
- **Number:** Multiple.
- **Distance:** Close.

Why would the author have written this story with this point of view? What are the possible benefits to this style?

In *No Mere Zombie*, Chris Fox has chosen to work with an ensemble cast of superheroes and supervillains that range from humans with military expertise to werewolves, zombies, and Egyptian gods. You may recall the discussion of how to choose the best point of view for a given scene in a multiple point of view story in chapter nine, "Keeping Them All Straight." Now that you've seen werewolves and zombies battling, let's analyze the point of view.

The first question we have to ask is why the ensemble cast? The story is large in scope, spanning several camps of heroes and villains. The action crosses the globe, then time, space, and dimensions. At a minimum, we could make a case for needing one point of view character per camp. Members of those camps don't stay together every minute of the day. They have their various missions, allegiances, and intrigues, so it does make sense to have multiple point of view characters in each camp. This story is an example of when you "just gotta have 'em."

And with that decided, two factors become paramount. One, make each point of view character distinct from all the others. Readers should be able to tell your characters apart without names attached. Two, make sure you control the narrative so that transitions between each perspective are easy to follow. Besides being easy to track, each change needs to introduce something that advances the story and could not be told through any other perspective.

Note that Fox only has one point of view character per chapter. Those chapter breaks create the clearest delineation between perspectives for both the writer and reader. Those clear breaks are a real asset to us when controlling craft, helping us avoid point of view slips and sloppy transitions. They also provide the reader with a clear break in the text whenever a shift occurs, which helps him to track the story both mentally and emotionally.

Fox uses a close emotional distance between the narrator and point of view character. As seen in these excerpts, depending on the perspective we're in the effect is quite different. The narrator is the same authorial voice throughout, but the tone of Irakesh's chapter is distinct from both Steve's and Liz's. It would be a problem if the tone and psychic distance were consistent throughout, because Irakesh is an ancient god. He is impassive and has a different historical and cultural lens through which he views the world than the other characters.

Consider these narrative sentences in Irakesh's passage. "They crowded the inside of the hangar, packing the area between the odd metal conveyances that these moderns referred to as airplanes." And,

"The deathless he'd indicated stood at least seven feet tall, an extreme rarity in Irakesh's time. It was heavily muscled, probably a combatant in one of the games the moderns called sports." This narrative does an excellent job of conveying Irakesh's perspective.

Compare Irakesh's perspective to Liz's. "She landed in a crouch near the doorway her two companions had just disappeared through. Damn Blair and damn Steve for following him. If he wasn't already dead she was going to kill him. They should have attacked as a group, but those two school kids had rushed blindly ahead." It's the same narrative voice, but the perspective is Liz's.

In the close third, the point of view character's attitude, emotions, and physical experience shape the narrative just as they would in the first person narrative, and comparing Irakesh's chapter to Steve's or Liz's makes that especially apparent. Clearly, by writing in the close third, Fox is able to convey those attitudes to readers more effectively than in a distant narrative. Even the omniscient voice would not work as well here. The omniscient narrator is authorial through and through. While able to enter all the characters' heads, Fox would have had to rely on action, dialogue, and thoughts to convey each character's perspective. With the close third, the narrator can inhabit the various perspectives and the character's attitude infuses the narrative. If I may return to the analogy of the bread and spread: In the omniscient, the narrative voice would be plain bread through each chapter. In the close third, the narrative voice is the bread plus cheese for Irakesh, bread plus peanut butter for Steve, and bread plus jalapeño jam for Liz.

Find out about Chris Fox at the back of this book.

TOM REEVE'S *FULL COVERAGE*

Before reading this excerpt, you should know that Kyle is an assassin in a world where everyone takes body-enhancing drugs and has bioprinted body parts. He got booted from his insurance plan and his drugs are wearing off. Richelle is his one-night stand.

"Is there a Kyle Soliano there?" The woman asked. A glint from the grill on her teeth flashed across the fish eye lens.

Kyle glanced back at the locked door to his office as he scratched his legs. His survival instincts screamed for him to get a very large gun right now, but Richelle was still in his apartment.

"Who wants to know?" Kyle replied as he scratched at the top of his chest.

A second woman burst through the wall to the left side of his doorway, leaving a hole that reached from floor to ceiling. A forest of long blonde dreadlocks shot out from the top of her head and nearly rubbed against Kyle's ceiling. Bits of what used to be Kyle's wall got caught on the various skull shaped pins that adorned her blue leather jacket.

She flashed Kyle a chrome-toothed grin and it appeared that she had sharpened two of her teeth into fangs.

Maxine had long ago chosen the werewolf as her spirit animal. When another assassin made this the butt of a joke during a company meeting, Maxine spent the following night furiously sharpening her teeth into fangs. The next day, she tore out the man's jugular with her teeth, disposed of his head in the compost bin, and stole his chair.

"We're here to crush your head." Spoke the musclebound hulk in an unsettlingly deep yet polite tone. She punched Kyle right in the gut and sent him flying backwards down the hall towards his kitchen. These two were definitely taking some good drugs.

Kyle gasped for breath as he grabbed his chest. His ribs felt like they were on fire but he didn't feel any fractures. His newfound layer of fat had provided some cushioning. What little painkillers were still in his system managed to keep the pain from overwhelming him.

Richelle screamed and ran to far the corner of Kyle's bedroom as the smaller woman entered through the hole in the wall.

"Hey Enyo, is she on the list?" The giant blonde woman pointed back at Richelle with her thumb.

"Let me see." The shorter pale woman thumbed through her phone. "No, see Maxine, she's not on the posting. Leave her." She tucked her phone back into her pocket and the two of them headed for Kyle.

He scrambled to his feet and grabbed the silencer with hollow point bullets that he kept behind his fridge. The slide snapped a round into the chamber just as the large blonde woman came around the corner.

He fired a shot point blank into the forehead of the woman. The bullet failed to penetrate and instead just scraped some skin off, revealing the chrome sheen of metal beneath it.

They weren't wearing grills on their teeth; all of the bones in their bodies had been printed with a metal coating. Swapping one of the cell cartridges in a bioprinter for titanium or other alloys allowed for armor-plated bones, preventatively reinforced knees, built-in brass knuckles, and nipples with rings pre-installed.

As with many professional assassins, Kyle had tried metalizing his body parts at one point and he was not a fan of it. Having to be extra careful around metal detectors was bad enough, but having to remember to pop in a metallic suppository every day to replenish the metal that his body purged out of his system got old fast.

"Shit." Kyle said with a quiver in his voice. He lowered the barrel of his gun to take aim at her left eye. There wouldn't be any metal there to block a bullet getting to her brain. Before he could get a shot off, she clamped her thick and heavy hand around his gun barrel. Kyle could see the printed in steel knuckles protruding from the back of her hand. She ripped the slide off his gun and smiled at him as she tossed it behind her.

He threw a punch at her abdomen and his hand recoiled in pain. It was like punching the wall of a building.

Maxine threw a punch at Kyle. He dodged it and took a shot at her neck. It was softer there, but he still couldn't cause any damage. She recovered and tried to bring her fist down on Kyle's outstretched arm. He deflected the blow and leaned all of his body weight on her arm to drive it into the drain of his sink. With a precise flex of his right butt cheek Kyle hit the switch for the garbage disposal.

* * *

Three months later, Kyle sat at a table on the balcony of the newly opened Original Gus in San Francisco. The restaurant had taken over the location of a previous burger joint on the fifth floor above a clothing store. From the balcony seats, Kyle could see several blocks in each direction. The crisp late morning air pushed back and forth against the scent of freshly grilled burgers coming out of the restaurant.

"So these are all from the same cow?" Kira asked from the seat across from him.

Original Gus prided itself on exceptionally consistent taste regardless of location. To this end all of their burger meat was made from clones of the same cow, the original Gus. Religious scholars and philosophers continued to debate whether or not this meant that Gus was constantly being reborn only to die over and over or if each clone contained its own unique variant of Gus's soul. Regardless of the metaphysics of the matter, the result was a delicious burger patty that tasted just as delicious as the previous one every time.

"No, just clones of the same cow." Kyle looked out over the balcony with a pair of binoculars.

"So, it is the same cow then?"

"No, different individual cows. Just very identical ones."

Before you read on, take a minute to consider the passage and identify the point of view. Then consider how the point of view shapes the story and its effect on you as a reader. Make notes in your journal. Answer the questions below for yourself before reading my answers.

- **Person:** Third.
- **Tense:** Past.
- **Number:** Omniscient.
- **Distance:** Middle.

Why would the author have written this story with this point of view? What are the possible benefits to this style?

Tom Reeve's *Full Coverage* is a satire about an assassin without insurance coverage. As such, a middle distance works well. We engage with Kyle, the protagonist, enough to like him and follow him on his misadventures, but we aren't too wrapped up in his psyche, and his emotional world is rather shallow, especially at the beginning of the story. This suits a story that expects us to laugh at our hero's mistakes and his resulting pain.

The narrator is an essayist-omniscient narrator. This is, again, a suitable choice for a satire. The story may appear to be a single point of view narrative, because the narrator is true to one point of view character, Kyle, and does not enter other character's perspectives. But the narrator is clearly omniscient, because he is able to tell us about other characters' backstories. He also makes observations outside the scope of the story and Kyle's knowledge base. He does so with a rather deadpan personality. Deadpan or not, it is a personality, and therefore an essayist, not authorial, narrator. The interjections about Maxine's werewolf spirit animal, metal-enhanced bones, and the original Gus are examples of this narrator's omniscience. He pauses the action to share information with the reader. If the essayist interjections detracted from the action they would not work, but we don't mind this pause, because the result is always humorous, as well as enlightening.

Why might Reeve have taken this approach? Because it suits the story he is telling very well. The story is billed as an action comedy, and one way to infuse the action with comedy is by sharing humorous observations with the reader during each scene, something Kyle probably could not do while getting beat up, but the narrator can and does. Surely it was fun to come up with outlandish, yet plausible in this world, situations to present the reader. We have just identified reasons of craft, audience, and artistry.

Find out about Tom Reeve at the back of this book.

ALIDA WINTERNHEIMER'S "LOVER"

Published in *Melusine* 3.1, Spring/Summer 2011

Your lover looks like a man of distinction, a man with enough money to content you in the world of things, the world of the worldly: world travel, exotic trinkets, foreign caviar, vintage wine, and designer gowns. Your lover has mostly gray hair, but he has all of his hair. When the white beard comes in after a weekend away from the city, you rub his chin with the flat of your hand, and the bristles scrape (up) then smooth (down) as you rub. He likes it when you do this because you are looking at him closely, inspecting him, and in your eyes, he sees that you regard him affectionately. Your lover has three names printed on his business cards. You will later reflect that it is a thin line between distinction and pretention, between classy and ostentatious, though at first you found it attractive and thought it boded well for yourself.

You feel that "boyfriend" is a juvenile word, while "lover" is a mature word. Because you have taken a lover, you feel grown up and possibly a little foreign, specifically French. You take to watching films that center on lovers: Henry and June, The Unbearable Lightness of Being, Little Children. You realize that these films are based on literary works of fiction. You are not incapable of enjoying literary fiction— you have read A Sport and a Pastime—but you absorb words without visualizing them; they are more like texture than color, so you watch the films and consume with your eyes the physicality of bodies together. You watch these films on the nights that you are alone. You will later reflect that "lover" is a word for the noncommittal. "Lover" implies sex and danger. Everything else—romance, adventure, exotica and erotica—can all be subsumed under sex and danger. With that understanding, "lover" seems like an insult.

Your lover does not want to meet your friends. Meeting your family is out of the question. You begin to lead two lives:

the old life that includes work, family, friends, friends to a diminishing extent; and the new life that fixates on your lover. Does he demand this of you? Perhaps, but you give yourself so willingly it hardly feels like a demand, something forced upon you. No, it seems like a necessity. If you are to love your lover, then you must be exclusive with your time, your energy, your face, your breath even. Your friends call you less than they used to. They have resigned themselves to waiting for you to get back to them as you have resigned yourself to evenings spent alone. Alone because you have made yourself available and he has remained unavailable. It is a necessity, you tell yourself. It frees you up for watching films about lovers. You begin to notice that the characters in the films usually come to violent harm, whether physical or emotional.

Your lover tells you that he loves you, but he could never give up his current commitments. He wants you to be his forever, even though he could never be yours, not fully. Do you love me? he wants to know. Do you love me? If so, then we have to make our time and space and it has to be enough. We have to carve it out from the rest of our lives and blossom within that niche. The idea of your love being confined to a niche depresses you. You feel like you have become a niche. His niche. But for what? What is he so carefully depositing there? You realize no one is really happy in those films.

You pack your suitcase with a strapless sundress and entirely new underwear. You are excited. This feels like fruition. Your lover noticed your despondency and showed you a plane ticket that he would not let you touch, to tease you. He is taking you away, somewhere exotic and hot. Perhaps the Riviera. Perhaps Italy. You once told him you had always wanted to ride a camel, so it may be Egypt. He tells you to pack lightly. He will buy you clothing there. You know it is across an ocean. This feels like a niche you can live with. You fly into Marrakech and spend a week eating olives and figs, wearing thin cotton dresses around the hotel and brightly colored tunics in the city. You wrap your hair in a turban and ride a camel. The camel feels like something you have known before. Your lover has fulfilled one of your dreams. You make love with the balcony doors open. The climate requires that you sweat behind your knees and in each other's arms, dampening the linens. When you go home, you ache for what you left behind. The first night you are alone, you masturbate. You find yourself weeping, and yet your resolve to continue has been deepened. You eat couscous every day for two weeks.

Your friends, those who have not drifted away entirely, are asking about your lover. You don't even have a photograph to show them. You have been insisting that you are in love with your lover for almost two years, and only now do you begin to realize that it is strange, his absence from the majority of your life. You feel your world contracting, as though the relationship is a box (niche) with shrinking walls. You realize it is your own desire that put you in this box, but you had not foreseen the distancing of yourself from everything else that you had been. Dissatisfaction creeps into your encounters. You begin to identify with the tragic lovers.

You tell him you cannot go on this way. He tells you to date other men. It will be good for you. Blindly, you try this. You tell the men willing to date you that you are in an open relationship. They are the sort of men who don't mind arrangements. Later, you will realize that while the relationship was open, it was mostly closed. You will feel bizarrely disconnected from two years of your life. You will think, I was a tragic lover. You cannot stand films (or literature) about lovers any more.

Before you read on, take a minute to consider the passage and identify the point of view. Then consider how the point of view shapes the story and its effect on you as a reader. Make notes in your journal. Answer the questions below for yourself before reading my answers.

- **Person:** Second (single, not plural).
- **Tense:** Present.
- **Number:** Omniscient.
- **Distance:** Distant.

Why would the author have written this story with this point of view? What are the possible benefits to this style?

Second person can be awkward to read and it is almost certainly uncomfortable. When we read first person, we understand that we are slipping into the personality of another, and we don't take all those

"I" pronouns personally. Yet, when we read "you" on the page, it's a form of direct address that can feel like an accusation. Because of the inherent discomfort, I kept the story very short; it's only 1,035 words and is reprinted here in its entirety.

I chose second person because I wanted the exploration of this character's situation—taking a lover who isolates her from her friends and family—to be uncomfortable for the reader. It also has the potential to make the reader consider whether or not she would ever find herself in this situation. It is easy to believe you would never do something until confronted with it.

Because the story is about intimacy and how one kind of intimacy can damage another kind of intimacy, I chose the singular person. If I had been addressing a collective second person point of view, the discomfort felt by the reader would be diluted. Just as if a group of school children are caught playing a prank, they can blame the others more than themselves, as though their participation in the prank was not really their own doing.

The narrator has knowledge of the future, beyond the scope of the story, which means she's omniscient. Interestingly enough, if this were a first person story, the narrator, being the character, would simply be telling the story from a point in the future at which time she could look back on these events with hindsight. In the first person, telling us what "you" will think later is a matter of lived experience, not prescience.

I chose the authorial-omniscient narrative voice for this piece because it works in juxtaposition to the subject matter. You might expect the character of the story to be overwrought with emotion— frustrated one day, consumed by passion the next. Distance will reveal that this is a rather sad time in her life. She thinks it's thrilling, but actually, she's spending most of her time alone, waiting for the passion, isolating herself from many for the sake of one. The narrative voice reflects this emotional bleakness, contrasting the character's reality to her perception.

In these four excerpts, we've seen examples of the first person, distant point of view in Artra's framing passage; close, single, third person point of view in Artra's main story; multiple, close, third person point of view in Fox's excerpts; middle, third person, essayist-omniscient point of view in Reeve's comedy; and distant, second person, authorial-omniscient point of view in my flash fiction piece. Combined with all the other examples in this book, you've explored and analyzed a wide a variety of points of view.

Chapter 16

Problems with Point of View (And How to Fix Them)

This chapter is a reference section to help you quickly identify and solve some of the big challenges with point of view.

1. Can I Tell This Story, *Please*?

Is your story primarily dialogue? Is your point of view character not letting your narrator speak? Are you unsure whether your narrator is a character or a voice? When writers aren't sure how to write narrative, they can develop a hulking point of view character and a ninety-eight pound weakling narrator. If your character is kicking sand in your narrator's face, you've got a POV stranglehold.

The Fix:

Step back and examine the point of view of your story. Look at person, number, and distance. You have four main choices for your narrative:

1. A first person narrator, who is by definition the point of view character as well, is telling the story as "I" from a point in time after the events of the story have occurred. The exception to this is the first person, present tense narrator, who is telling the story while it occurs.

2. The subjective narrator of a close, third person point of view, who is like the first person narrator in distance, bias, and scope of knowledge, but is an authorial voice, not a character's, outside the action of the story.

3. The authorial-omniscient narrator, who is the classic narrative voice associated with the author. The authorial narrator will be impartial in the telling of the story.

4. The essayist-omniscient narrator, who is a persona of the author. The essayist need not be impartial toward the characters and events he's describing.

Once you've figured out who your narrator is and how much she knows, notice all the things the narrator does that the point of view character can't or won't. Now give your narrator a booster shot and a bullhorn. In revision, flesh out the story with the appropriate narrative exposition.

For more help, revisit Chapter 4, Heart Your Narrator.

2. Short-Sighted and Far-Reaching

Writers tend to favor a close narrative distance. This can create problems when the distance is too close, squeezing out intricacies within the story that the reader needs to see. Or when the distance never varies and the voice and mood become monotonous. Distance is multifaceted, and like perspective in a painting or the camera angle in film, it is something writers can use to shape a desired effect on the reader.

The Fix:

Practice writing in various points of view, changing the physical distance, emotional and psychic distance, and chronological distance from one scene to the next. Choose a set of parameters, such as an authorial omniscient narrator, with a close psychic distance between reader and character. Write a scene in which you practice changing the physical distance between the narrative lens and the action. Or try a limited, third person narrator, emotionally distant from the point of view character and write a scene that is emotionally intense for the character. To refresh your understanding of psychic distance, review the examples with Reverend Hansen in chapter five, "Don't Stand So Close to Me."

For more help, revisit Chapter 5, Don't Stand So Close to Me.

3. People Leave before the Party's Over

When a reader opens the covers of a book, it's important to make what's inside inviting, so she'll find a chair and settle in for a good read. Hooking the reader with some intriguing action is only part of it. If readers who stick around love your story, but their numbers are few, the problem might be with your point of view.

The Fix:

Be aware of how much information you present to the reader in your opening passage. The narrative voice, mood, point of view character, and your control over all those elements will be presented to any reader in the first few paragraphs of your story. Study other people's work. Notice whether the writer is in control of his opening or if he expects the reader to get through too much set up and world building before getting into the story. The latter can be like hitting a speed bump on the way to the freeway.

Regardless of genre or style, your opening must be an honest representation of what is to come. A slapdash opening won't win readers. A bait and switch will anger readers. There is no trick to writing a solid opening; you simply need to give it the time and attention it deserves. And be certain the point of view comes shining through.

For more help, revisit Chapter 6, Making Introductions.

4. I Did That on Accident

When you don't make any attempt to control your story's point of view, you end up with an accidental narrative. Accidents often include lots of slips, a lack of distinctive narrative voice, lack of a clear protagonist with multiple point of view characters, and a sloppy or meandering story.

The Fix:

If you aren't sure why you're writing in a specific point of view, take a hard look at it. You should be able to explain what this point of view adds to the reader's experience of your story.

Are there reasons of craft and the story's structure that make this point of view the best one? Or can you think of another point of view that better supports your story's structure? If that first person narrator isn't able to handle the job, take it over yourself. Switch to an authorial third person.

Answer these questions:

- What effect do you want the point of view to have on the reader?
- What goals do you have for your own creative process and artistry?

If you are working in the right point of view, you may need to exercise more control so it works *for* you and your story. If you've discovered that another point of view would be better, you've made an important discovery. Write on!

For more help, see Chapter 7, The Right Point of View.

5. Traveling Through Hyper-reality

If you're truly dedicated to your point of view character's perspective, you might find yourself ruining the pace of your story and boring your reader. Whether you're writing a traveling chapter in real time or filling every scene with the tiniest of details, providing a hyper-real experience on the page is simply *too much*. You probably wouldn't regale your friends with tales of brushing your teeth and filling your cereal bowl, so don't try to pass it off as story with your readers.

The Fix:

When your story is hyper-real, step back from that point of view character and let your narrator take the reins. Your narrator can use exposition and summary to move the character and reader through the story without getting stuck in minutiae. He can also bend and fold time as needed—that's what scene and chapter breaks are for.

If, for some reason, you really want to show that character filling his cereal bowl, define how that action advances plot, character, or theme. Then make sure the reader will get it. In other words, filling the cereal bowl has to be about something other than filling the cereal bowl, something intrinsic to your plot, character, or theme.

For more help, revisit Chapter 8, He Said, She Said.

6. Slipups

When the perspective slips into a head it doesn't belong in, you've committed a point of view slip. If you're writing anything but omniscient, there will be characters who do not have a point of view. Entering one of those heads is called a slip, and it is conspicuous. It jumps off the page at the reader who has become accustomed to the rules of the story.

For example, if you ruled that only Simona, Peter, and Gemma get a point of view, the reader becomes used to that. Furthermore, if you determined that there is only one point of view per chapter, the reader gets used to that, too. Say you are in a Simona chapter and you slip into Peter's head, telling something only Peter could know. The reader will notice because it breaks the pattern, and she will be jarred out of the story.

The Fix:

Be an attentive reader of your own work. When you finish a draft, take a day or two off, then read it. The best thing is to print it out—sorry, trees—and read it on paper. Shift your mental focus from screen mode to the more leisurely mindset, away from your desk, of reading a book. You'll see things differently than when you read it on a screen. Once you spot the slip, fix it. That is why we have this thing called revision.

For more help, revisit Chapter 9, Keeping Them All Straight.

7. Leap Frog and Other Games

There are several common problems found in multiple point of view stories.

The easiest to identify is head hopping, when the point of view shifts rapidly, often unexpectedly, from one point of view character's perspective to another's.

Often with multiple point of view characters, some of those characters don't get the attention they deserve. They are left underdeveloped and can seem generic.

Using too many point of view characters can create spoilers by giving too much information to the reader.

The Fix:

The first, simplest, and often best remedy for all of the issues above is to kill your darlings. Axe as many point of view characters as you can. The remaining point of view character will create a set of useful parameters for your story, and you will avoid any previous errors by being true to your one and only point of view.

When you must have more than one point of view character, create a hierarchy and clear rules for when to use which perspective and how to shift between them. Following those rules—rules of your own creation—will help you create robust characters who deserve their crowns.

You can find the Choose the Right Point of View Character worksheet at www.WordEssential.com/JoinStoryWorksPOV.

For more help, revisit Chapter 9, Keeping Them All Straight.

8. The Faulty Crystal Ball

Sometimes writers write without deciding if they are writing a multiple, third person point of view or an omniscient one. When you aren't clear yourself, how can you expect your writing to be true to one or the other? This results in shifts in perspective that do not fit with the whole, changes in voice that confuse the reader, and other slipups that, because they are accidental, call attention to themselves.

The Fix:

To test whether you should write in the omniscient, ask yourself:

- Does my narrator need the power to enter any character's head? Or the setting? Or props?
- Does my narrator need to make connections outside the realm of possibility for the characters?
- Does my narrator need to reference the past or future beyond the bounds of the story?

If so, you need an omniscient narrator, but then you must make your narrator omniscient through and through. It's not enough to offer only a glimpse of this power; it will read as a mistake that you made in handling your narrative.

For more help, revisit Chapter 10, Playing God.

9. Nobody Here but Me

When writing a first person narrative, writers often forget they need to have a narrator at all. Even in a first person, present tense point of view, the character must fulfill the duties of narrator or the story will be anemic, reading like a script with dialogue, stage directions, and the occasional soliloquy.

The Fix:

Before you begin writing a first person narrative, make sure your character can handle the duties of narrative exposition well enough to satisfy your reader.

Decide who your narrator is. Yes, it is your first person character, but it is this character at a later stage in life, one who has gained perspective and hindsight on the events of the story. Also, decide to whom your narrator is telling the story. What tone are you trying to establish? How intimate is the conversation between narrator and audience? Picture your character telling the story to a particular person. The tone will change if that person is her doctor, her favorite teacher, or her dead sister.

Knowing those things and fixing them in your mind will help you fulfill *your* narrative duties and will shape the voice, perspective, and level of intimacy that the narrator shares with the audience.

For more help, revisit Chapter 11, It's Mine, All Mine.

10. The One, Two, Reveal

If you're writing an unreliable narrator, things can get confusing pretty fast. You've got to keep multiple storylines going in your mind, figure out when to hint and what to reveal when, and create an exciting reveal that will surprise and delight readers. How are you going to keep it all straight?

The Fix

The first thing you need to figure out is why your narrator is unreliable. His motivation is the fuel for the narrative engine. Whether it's psychosis or grief, once you know what is compelling the lies, you'll have a sense of how to shape them on the page. Is the narrator malicious and deceitful? Or is he deceiving himself as well as the reader?

Just as many writers like to write the climax and then plot up to it, it's a good idea to craft the big reveal early—if not while storyboarding, then in the first draft. Once the big reveal is established, you'll be able to lay in appropriate clues while you write and revise. A clue is anything that begins to not add up as the story progresses, which will fall into place for the reader after the reveal.

In the case of he said, she said stories, clues will also include discrepancies between the characters' version of events. If you present both versions to the reader, it is done so in order raise intrigue. Was Carole mad enough to kill Dick? Or was she so distraught that a loss of control led to a tragic accident?

Carefully structuring the narrative is critical to an unreliable narrator story. A useful way to prepare for writing your own is to read stories known for their unreliable narrators. Take the time as you read to mark up your copy of the book. Note any clues you find as you read it through, then go back post-reveal and look for any clues you missed while examining the structure of the story.

For more help, revisit Chapter 12 "Trust Me."

11. Who Let Him in Here, Anyway?

An unearned point of view can hurt your story. If the character's perspective doesn't advance the plot and increase the tension, it can slow your pacing. If he spoils your reveals, you might as well sit on one hand as you type the rest of your story. Those reveals are a writer's currency; spend them wisely and let no character spoil them. The character might be perfectly good and useful, but his perspective is clutter, bloating your manuscript.

The Fix:

Before handing out point of view crowns willy-nilly, ask if those characters have earned them:

- Is this character fully developed, likable and fascinating enough to carry a point of view?
- Is this perspective advancing the story toward a climax?
- Is this character adding a unique perspective to the events of the story?

If you answer no or aren't sure about any one of those, cut the character's perspective. By figuring out a way to show the events that were in that character's point of view without that perspective, you will refine your skills as a writer and take your manuscript to a new level.

If you're still unsure, answer this: "If I have to send Alida $50 for each point of view character I create, is this guy worth it?" I bet you'll find ways to be true to a single point of view character, or at least minimal perspectives, then take a writer out for dinner!

For more help, revisit Chapter 13, Earning Their Keep.

12. The Dread Info Dump

Info dumps happen to the best of us, but they are avoidable. Sometimes our narrators need to explain something so the reader understands the next crucial movement in the story. But a big, boring block of text is never the answer.

The Fix:

That information can be conveyed in a more meaningful way. You can

- spread the information out in a scene,
- use dialogue, or
- cut it and find another way to get the information to the reader.

Remember, the time to feed the reader information is never during a high-stakes action scene. Set up your action well before it happens, giving the information a scene of its own, if that's appropriate.

For more help, revisit Chapter 14, Don't Dump on Your Reader, or Your Reader Will Dump You.

13. Weak Effects

If you are not thinking about the effect you want to have on the reader in any given scene, you are likely to miss an opportunity to craft the most compelling work of fiction you possibly can.

The Fix:

When you sit down to write, know what kind of scene you're writing, how it advances your plot arc, character arc, and themes. Then ask yourself how you intend to affect the reader with this scene.

It is your job as writer to shape the material on the page in such a way that the reader is moved and therefore compelled to keep turning your pages. The emotional effect could range from quiet contemplation to rage. It is desirable for any book to create a range of emotion. Just as you would not want to listen to a one-note song for very long, one emotional note in a story does not a story make.

Once you have identified your desired effect on the reader, create a sense of connection between the reader and the character, and use sensory details in the *now*-action of the scene.

For more help, revisit Chapter 15, Effectively Affecting Your Reader.

Now that you've read *The Story Works Guide to Writing Point of View,* and have completed all the exercises, you know how to harness the power of point of view and write amazing narratives.

It begins with an understanding of the relationship between the author, narrator, point of view character, and reader and ends with a masterfully crafted story.

My last piece of advice to you is to play with your point of view. Take the time to discover the best combination of elements for your story. By doing this, you'll be assured that you are playing to your and your story's strengths. And those strengths will grow with every page you write!

Get Your Bonus

Thank you for reading *The Story Works Guide to Writing Point of View!*

Get three special episodes of the Story Works Round Table. In these conversations about craft, Alida and her co-hosts, Kathryn and Robert, discuss why writers struggle with narrative (Chapter 4), the pros and cons of ensemble cast fiction (Chapter 9), and the fun challenge of writing an unreliable narrator (Chapter 12).

www.WordEssential.com/StoryWorksPOVBonus

While you're there, don't forget to join the mailing list.
www.WordEssential.com/JoinStoryWorksPOV

You'll receive a downloadable Choose the Right Point of View Character worksheet to help you navigate multiple point of view stories.

You'll also:

- receive Alida's newsletter and the Story Works Round Table podcast,
- be notified when future books in The Story Works Guide to Writing Fiction Series come out,
- be the first to hear about writing courses, and
- get special offers.

Don't forget the cool factor!

Acknowledgments

I feel incredibly blessed to do what I do and am grateful to the many wonderful people in my life, especially my editing and coaching clients.

From our first days at Hamline, Nicodemus Taranovsky has been a tremendous source of support and wise counsel. Nico is the first person I send my work, the one I call when I get stuck, and I can't wait for our next journey to the "other side!"

Bryan Cohen, Chris Fox, and Robert Scanlon have been constant sources of support and feedback. Our mastermind is a blessing, and I am truly grateful to count you among my friends.

To all of my editing and coaching clients who gave me permission to excerpt your work, thank you for your faith in me.

The Story Works Round Table podcast grew out of this craft book project. I have amazing co-hosts. Kathryn Arnold and Robert Scanlon bring intelligence, wit, and volumes of reading experience to each show. We truly have so much fun every time we sit down to talk craft. Find the show at www.StoryWorksPodcast.com.

To Leeland Artra, Aldus Baker, Chris Fox, Matt Herron, Tom Reeve, and Judy K. Walker, whose works are excerpted in this book, I am truly grateful for your contribution to this discussion of point of view. Your wonderful words are now helping other writers develop their craft.

The care and expertise of Daria Brannan, Jana Rade, and Dara Syrkin was invaluable as I turned this project into a book ready to enter the world and the hands of readers. I'm lucky to have found three such talented women to have on my team.

Contributing Writers

LEELAND ARTRA

Leeland Artra lives in the Emerald City (Seattle, Washington) with his amazingly patient wife and idea-inspiring son. The first half of his life was "wasted" (as his mother once said) avidly reading science-fiction/fantasy and role playing. He continues to improve his time-wasting skills daily. He does contribute to society as a software engineer most weekdays (which he calls being a code janitor) and does his best to avoid TV in the 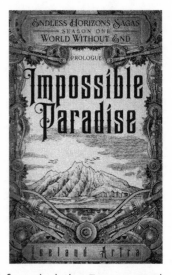 evenings by writing more books. Leeland founded the Fantasy and Science-Fiction Network. FSFNet is a cooperative support group for authors who write flinch-free fantasy or science fiction. FSFNet also promotes children's literacy worldwide at www.FSFNet.com. You can find Leeland at www.LArtra.com.

ALDUS BAKER

Aldus Baker lives in Kansas with his wife and children. He is currently working on the second novel in the Crown Saga, a young adult fantasy series, along with other writing projects. He is also a software developer and lives a somewhat normal life while trying to catch up on laundry. Some of the ideas in Hidden Ability had been kicking around inside his head for years. Now they are in a book for you to read and enjoy! You can find Aldus at www.AldusBaker.com.

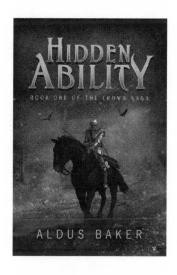

CHRIS FOX

Chris Fox has been writing since he was six years old and started inflicting his work on others at age eighteen. By age twenty-four, people stopped running away when he approached them with a new piece. Shortly thereafter, he published his first story in *The Rifter*. Chris lives in Novato, California with his wife, where he writes several successful science fiction and speculative fiction series, as well as a popular nonfiction series for writers. You can find Chris at www.ChrisFoxWrites.com.

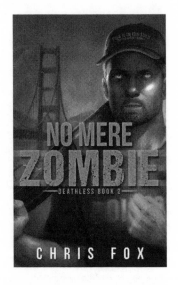

MATT HERRON

Born in 1988, M.G. Herron's full name is Matthew Gilbert Herron. He writes science fiction and fantasy novels and short stories. His first novel, *The Auriga Project*, was published in 2015. Books and reading have always been close to his heart. He loves epic fantasies and fast-paced action adventure novels. His passion for literature, the dusty vanilla smell of old paperbacks, and turns of phrase that prickle your skin eventually led him into writing, and he now earns his living as freelance writer and storyteller. He lives in Austin, Texas with his girlfriend, Shelly, and their dog, Elsa. You can find Matt at www.MGHerron.com.

TOM REEVE

Tom Reeve grew up in San Diego, California. He holds a BS from the University of California, Berkeley and an MS from the University of Michigan, both for Mechanical Engineering. He has worked primarily in the medical device industry since 2007 because it is challenging, weird and often very gross. He currently lives in San Francisco, California with an ever-rotating cast of roommates. When he isn't busy working or writing, Tom spends his time running marathons, going to random concerts, playing video games, and watching cheesy movies. You can find Tom at www.BooksByTomReeve.com.

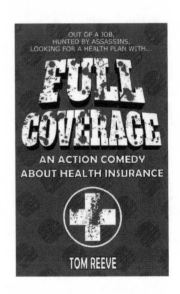

NICODEMUS WOLFGANG TARANOVSKY

Nicodemus Taranovsky lives in Saint Paul, Minnesota with his wife, Sharon, an abundance of cats, and a lone Italian Greyhound. When not writing, he is busy teaching with the Minnesota Prison Writing Workshop, reading, learning languages, cooking, gardening, playing Frisbee, or exploring the Twin Cities.

JUDY K. WALKER

Judy K. Walker is the author of the ongoing Sydney Brennan Mysteries series, set in Tallahassee, Florida. Her most recent release, *Prodigal,* is the first book in the Dead Hollow thriller trilogy. Set in a fictional Appalachian community, Judy had to reach far back into memory for the experience of changing seasons. She currently writes from rainy east Hawaii, where the seasons are defined by what type of tree is fruiting. You can find Judy at www.JudyKWalker.com.

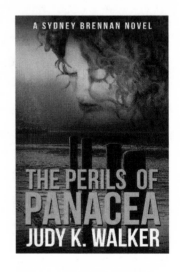

About the Author

Alida Winternheimer entered this world holding a mechanical pencil and sheaf of loose-leaf paper—at least, it seems that way to her. The book she couldn't do without is a blank one. With unlimited pages. Always hungry for knowledge, she has a Master of Fine Arts in Writing from Hamline University and a Master of Liberal Studies from the University of Minnesota. She happily shares the knowledge she's acquired as your writing coach at Word Essential. She hosts the Story Works Round Table podcast, where she gets to have conversations about craft with her amazing co-hosts.

She writes several genres, from fairy tale to literary, and edits all genres. To date, she has published three novels, two craft books, and multiple short stories, two of which were nominated for the Pushcart Prize. She is constantly thinking up new characters—living and dead—to inhabit her worlds.

She lives in the fabulous Minneapolis, Minnesota, with her golden retriever, Seva the Wonder Dog. When she's not writing, editing, or teaching, she facilitates Seva's career as a demonstration service dog, and likes to kayak or snowshoe, depending on the season. She also bikes, goes camping, feeds the animals, hugs the trees, and counts her lucky stars.

Please go to www.WordEssential.com/About to find more
information about Alida and her work.

If you'd like to contact Alida, send her a note at
Alida@WordEssential.com.

Glossary and Index

TERM	CHAPTER	PAGE	DEFINITION
Ambiguous ending	12	213	An open-ended conclusion to a story that leaves the reader to make a decision about the meaning or resolution of story events. Many readers find these endings uncomfortable.
Authorial-Omniscient narrator	10	156	The authorial-omniscient narrator is the classic literary storyteller. He is invisible, respectable, and formal. He narrates from on high. See also Essayist-Omniscient narrator and Omniscient.
Audience	4	37	The assumed readers of a book who share certain common traits, such as sympathy toward the protagonist, a love of action or romance, a preference for fast-pacing. To define your audience, ask, "What kind of reader will enjoy this story?"
Central first person narrator	11	181	The central first person narrator is the clear protagonist, getting in and out of trouble, at the center of the climax. See also Peripheral first person narrator.

TERM	CHAPTER	PAGE	DEFINITION
Character arc	8	122	The main character's internal change, or evolution, brought about by the events of the story. To have a complete arc, a character must be a different person at the end of the story than she was at the beginning. The character arc plus the chronological distance will shape the voice of a first person narrative.
Distance	3/5	24/67	Distance refers to the sense of distance between the narrator or the reader and both the point of view character and the events of the story. The author manipulates distance to affect how the narrator tells the story and how the reader receives the story. There are several kinds of distance that work together to create your chosen effects. They are physical, emotional, psychic, and chronological. Distance is referred to as close or distant, and sometimes middle.
Essayist-Omniscient narrator	10	156	The essayist-omniscient narrator is a personal storyteller, with a noticeable presence on the page. He exercises his opinions and freely passes judgment. See also Authorial-Omniscient narrator.
Head hopping	9	131	Head hopping is a phenomenon in which the point of view jumps, froglike, from one character to another without reason or control.

TERM	CHAPTER	PAGE	DEFINITION
Hook	6	98	An open, or unresolved, question at the open of a book, end of a chapter, or end of a book in a series that entices the reader to continue reading.
Identification to opposition	5	83	The relationship between reader and point of view character can be placed on a spectrum from identification to opposition, which answers the question, "To what extent will your reader feel at one with the character?"
Info dump	14	229	When the narrator tries to explain something to the reader and does so in a block of text. Often it is exposition about a setting, a technology, or a concept that has to be explained for the reader to progress in the story. An info dump can also take the shape of a character telling us too much information, information we can glean in subtle and more meaningful ways.
Intrigue	9	137	Questions the writer expects a reader to ask as she reads the story, because of the specific material on the page. E.g. If this character has anxiety around water, then the reader will wonder what happened to her involving water. Questions raised as intrigue are eventually addressed in a series of reveals or a big reveal. See also Reveal.

TERM	CHAPTER	PAGE	DEFINITION
Juxtaposition	4	42	Juxtaposition occurs when you place two elements together in a scene that oppose or contrast each other in order to heighten the desired effect upon the reader.
Limited point of view	3	24	In a limited point of view, the narrator's knowledge, and therefore her capacity to report information to the reader, is limited to what the point of view character can know. See also Omniscient.
Narrative	4	35	The textual element of the story that is aware of the reader and ensures the story is told in a rich, engaging manner. That narrative will have a voice of its own, distinct from the point of view character's voice. The narrative voice defines the style of the piece. We can attribute the narrative voice to the narrator. See also Narrative exposition and Narrator.
Narrative exposition	4	39	Narrative exposition provides the reader with all elements of the story that the point of view character, who is busy acting, cannot or will not be able to incorporate into the story via his perspective. See also Narrative, Narrator, and Summary.

TERM	CHAPTER	PAGE	DEFINITION
Narrator	4	37	Your narrator is the teller of the story and may be the voice of the author, the author's persona, or a character on the page. See also Narrative and Narrative exposition.
Number	3	23	How many perspectives the narrator can enter over the course of the story. A single point of view means we only experience one character's perspective. A multiple point of view means we experience two or more characters' perspectives. An omniscient point of view means the narrator can enter all of the characters' perspectives.
Omniscient	3	23	The omniscient narrator can enter all the characters' perspectives. Omniscient narrators refer to characters in the third person. Also, the narrator is not bound by the laws of space or time. She can flash forward and backwards beyond the lifetime of characters, can relate one character's experience to another's in ways the characters themselves cannot, and can even enter the perspective of the setting, the props, and the universe at large. See also Authorial-Omniscient narrator, Essayist-Omniscient narrator, and Limited point of view.

TERM	CHAPTER	PAGE	DEFINITION
Peripheral first person narrator	11	181	The peripheral first person narrator is involved in the trouble and the climax, but is telling someone else's story. Yet through this involvement and telling, he becomes a different person. See also Central first person narrator.
Person	3	22	Person is identified by the pronoun used in the story's narrative. A story may be told in the first, second, or third person and the singular or plural. Third person is the most common. First person is second most common. Other variations are seldom used.
Point of view	3	21	The narrative constructs, or conceptual elements, through which a reader experiences the story. See also Point of view character.
Point of view character	3	21	The reader experiences the story through this character's perspective. Every story is shaped by the perspective through which it is told. See also Point of view.
POV stranglehold	4	47	POV stranglehold occurs when the writer is committed to putting on the page only what the point of view character can see, smell, touch, taste, hear, and infer, essentially choking off the narrator.

TERM	CHAPTER	PAGE	DEFINITION
Reveal	9	129	Transitive verb: the process of exposing information to the reader. Noun: The moment of "the reveal" when the writer answers questions the reader has been led to ask. These questions are referred to as intrigue. These answers are often found in a character's backstory. See also Intrigue.
Show/Showing	4	39	Showing is a narrative style that engages the reader's senses and emotions through specific details. See also Tell/Telling.
Spectacle	15	252	When you write trauma into your story without giving the reader time to bond with your point of view character, you create spectacle. See also Tragedy.
Stakes	9	142	Stakes are what the character stands to gain or lose as a result of mounting trouble. Stakes escalate as the story nears the climax, creating the rise in the plot arc. See also Tension.

TERM	CHAPTER	PAGE	DEFINITION
Summary	4	45	A form of narrative exposition used when you need to show the passage of time or distance, or some activity the character must do that is not really story-worthy. Summary gives the reader what she needs to know without slowing the pace of the story. See also Narrative exposition.
Tell/Telling	4	39	A weak narrative style in which the writer talks about, explains things to, or slips into anecdotal writing. Telling creates flat prose that fails to engage the reader's imagination. See also Show/Showing.
Tense	3	23	Tense simply identifies whether a story is told in the past or present tense.
Tension	9	142	What the reader feels when there is an unresolved question implied by the story, both through the action and the relationships on the page. As stakes increase for the character, the reader feels increasing concern over the outcome. See also Stakes.
Tragedy	15	253	When you write trauma into your story after the reader has developed a connection with your point of view character, you create tragedy. See also Spectacle.

TERM	CHAPTER	PAGE	DEFINITION
Twist	12	213	A surprising change in the story that comes as a moment of shocking realization for the reader. What the reader thought she knew is suddenly given new meaning.
Unreliable narrator	12	196	A narrator whose veracity, motives, and character are brought into question through inconsistencies in the point of view or through one or more characters' perspectives. The resulting effect upon the reader is destabilizing, precisely because she can't bring herself to trust the narrator.
Voice	4	41	The underlying tone of the story that does not change, no matter the setting or point of view. The voice of the piece will make it a cohesive whole, not just a string of related events and characters.

List of Exercises

Made in the USA
Middletown, DE
23 December 2017